To You.

THE AVERAGE BROKEN MAN

I WILL ALWAYS LOVE YOU!
UNCONDITONALLY! SHINE BRIGHT
MY ANGEL.!

x x

THE AVERAGE BROKEN MAN

ONE MAN'S STORY OF EVERYDAY LIFE TRYING TO UNDERSTAND

THE STRUGGLES IN RELATIONSHIPS, EMOTIONAL PAIN, FEAR, ANXIETY,

DEPRESSION, LOVE,ACCEPTANCE, VALIDATION AND HEALING

THROUGH A SPIRITUAL AWAKENING

DEDICATED TO MY DAUGHTER

I dedicate this book to you, so that as you live your life, you can do so from a place of knowing where, why, and how you became the person you are today.

Life at times is a hard and cruel place to be. You will have your own challenges and trauma to deal with, as you are on your own journey.

I hope that with me sharing my truth and vulnerability, it gives you the answers you are seeking to some of the feelings and emotions you have felt growing up and are yet to face in years to come.

I see that despite of all the pain and hurt I may have caused you at times, there was a reason behind it that, I simply did not understand or know why I was showing up the way I was in your life – but now I do.

I am sorry for the times I made you cry. I am sorry for the times I walked away from you and I am sorry you had to see and witness the separation of the two people who love you more than anything else.

This happened because neither me or your mum were conscious of our own programmes or patterns and despite our best efforts, there was nothing we could have done to fix this. The universe simply had to step in and make one of us see the lessons we needed to learn.

I love you with everything that I am, and there are not enough words I can express just how happy I am to know that because of my journey I can now help you with yours. I will stand by you every step of the way.

I have got your back! **LOVE DAD X**

CONTENTS

THE "JUICE"

ENVIRONMENT

APPROVAL

GIVING & RECEIVING LOVE

FEARFUL AVOIDANCE

ACCEPTANCE

SHAME & GUILT

ATTATCHEMENTS

CURIOSITY & DENIAL

RESPONSIBILITIES

FAMILY SEPERATION

SELFWORTH

MEN

TRUTH & AUTHENTICITY

ACKNOWLEDGEMENTS

REFERENCES

JOURNAL & NOTES SECTION

I am not a leading figure in the world of self-improvement, nor am I a celebrity with a million followers on Instagram or a YouTube channel. I am not the director or CEO of some large company or corporate business, but I am not on my arse either.

What I am is the average man. The kind of man you see walking past you in the street, the guy at the supermarket, the guy in the office you work with or the guy sat next to you in his car waiting in a queue of traffic trying to get somewhere. The man who dreads going home to his family and kids, the man fearful of what the future holds. The man worried everyday if he is loved by his partner, his kids, and whether he is enough. I can say that without doubt that every man on this planet has an element of worry, fear of acceptance or value. How many of those men that you see every day in your life do you think would openly speak up about their truths, their pain, their feelings or what they were going through? Well, I do not know the answer, but I would say it is probably less than 1%.

Would me telling you that I am a fallen soldier crippled with PTSD from years in combat haunted by all the mental scars of war and savagery witnessed, make this more of an interesting read? Would me telling you that I was once an A-list celebrity fallen from grace and public approval to nothing, gripped by the addiction of drugs, drink or sex scandals, trying to stay on top and in the public eye make this a more touching read? Or would me telling you I am a 30-year-old established psychology professor with years of academic research under my belt, make this a more validating read? Well, I guess you are going to be disappointed then if that's what you were hoping for.

I am none of these people but, what I am is **THE AVERAGE MAN**!

I do not have a tragic story to tell you. I have not suffered major adversity in life, nor have I had to overcome extreme difficulties that most would perceive as life struggles. I was not raised by an alcoholic father who beat me, or a mother who had me adopted because she was not able to cope with motherhood at an early age. I have not been in the care system trying to find my place in the world or a sense of purpose or belonging. I have not suffered sexual or physical abuse at any stage in my life and although each of these life stories is horrific and very real for many, and I do feel deeply for each one that has suffered from such events, that is precisely the whole purpose of this book. You do not need to have suffered major trauma in life to justify your suffering. Yes, most trauma does impact us. It is proven scientifically and through years of research but even the slightest misguided experience can hold deep roots and subconscious patterns that most of us do not know are even within us.

The average man has an equally hard battle with life but how many people would see this, acknowledge it, or even realize it. Most of these experiences are in the dark deep depths of our subconscious mind, and never really experienced in the day to day or in the three-dimensional reality we all live in. We think we are living a normal existence of who we are, but the sad reality is that not many of us are living authentically and very few of us are truly self-aware to the point where we can make better choices and decisions that will improve our lives for the better. The mental health in men at this present time seems to be at an all-time high and considered one of the biggest factors in male suicide and it's growing exponentially.

How many times have the rich and famous reached out with their status to get men to "open up" and talk about their feelings, how they are coping, express how life is treating them? How many times have you heard someone say, "that blokes' got issues"? How many national campaigns are pushed out into the world asking men to come forward, even the young Royals are at it, just to gain some traction on this ever-growing and widening issue. How many wives, partners, friends and family have taken the time to reach out to the men in their lives and ask, "are you ok"? Furthermore, how many women would be able to listen to the men in their lives and support them from a place of non-judgement and acceptance and not from their own insecurities and fears of losing that stability they currently have with their significant other? It is commonly believed that women are raised with the preconceived idea and expectations that men should be strong, dependable, stable, loyal, supportive and above all else be there for them when they need them.

The minute the man in her life begins to struggle she sees a weakness, or that he lacks any form of compassion or affection and he comes across as if he does not care or is simply not interested. Rejection and fears that the relationship is going nowhere start to creep in and she is looking to jump ship. The fact is that all men are shit-scared and afraid to show any form of vulnerability and be honest about true feelings with their partners. We live in fear that if we do, she will want to leave us, reject us, judge us, devalue our worth and simply stop loving us. This leads to all sorts of relationship issues, ultimately leading to the end of what was previously an extraordinarily strong loving union or partnership we devote ourselves to. The lack of open communication about feelings from men and the willingness for women to accept these weaknesses from the men in their lives is the biggest social issue we have all been programmed with subconsciously.

Now, before you get all judgemental with me and say women also have mental health issues so why the bias? This book is for both men and women.

Sadly, what I will share in this book equally affects both sexes and there is no getting away from that fact. It is widely acknowledged that women generally have more empathy and can share more emotionally than men, hence the disparity between women and men in relationships. It has never been socially acceptable for men to show vulnerability or weakness, it is just not in our DNA.

The hunter gatherer or caveman mentality has haunted man for thousands of years and has passed down the generations in programming and experiences that have shaped our subconscious mind. The simple fact is that most men do not do emotions. I hope that by me sharing my story as the average man, it will encourage more men to share, be vulnerable and speak their truth. To take a long hard look at your life and experiences that you have been a part of, felt or seen and allow yourself to reflect and go back and accept the feelings and emotions of these life events. It is not a comfortable place to go to and most will not in fear of showing vulnerability and emotion. I guess the buzz word of the moment is "that it's OK not to be OK".

I trust this book will give you an insight into just how much pain your husband, boyfriend or significant other might be going through. They, like me, were once crippled with fear about being vulnerable to the people in my life and the woman I loved. My story might just be the key to help you understand why your significant other is showing up the way he or she is with you and why your relationship is causing pain and misery and lack of clarity on what to do about it. It might help you understand your patterns and allow you to make different choices.

What inspired me to write this was the eventual failure of my relationship with a woman I loved for seventeen years. My story is probably no different to every other man's story on some level. We have all lost someone we love and battled extreme pain for the loss it causes and the fallout from divorce or separation. It influences the family, the kids, the cat, the dog - everyone gets affected by it. Granted everyone has their own story as we are all different, but I wanted to understand how and why this happened to me and the reasons for the pain, suffering and hurt I have experienced in my life within relationships and why I was never able to fully accept love or give love unconditionally.

Like I said, I am not professing this is the answer. There are hundreds of different reasons for the way men and women equally show up in relationships that fail, but this is my journey and if just one man or woman can take something from my experience and avoid what I went through then this book was worth the effort. In a way it also gives me a sense of validation that my journey through the pain and suffering was worth it and that I am now on the right path to finding that true unconditional love we all strive for.

CHAPTER 1

ENTERING THE WORLD

Born in Mexico City on January 11th, 1974 to English parents, a month premature and by emergency procedure, at the time considered very high risk, now run of the mill, the (c - section) due to being in breach, my entrance into this world was not the greatest of starts. Having the umbilical cord wrapped around my neck was not the way it was supposed to be. Two days in intensive care without physical contact with my mother was probably the first issue that would affect my subconscious psyche in years to come, who knows, but let us continue.

My father was raised predominantly by his mother as his father was not present, apart from in his early years, but then left never to be seen again. My father has told me the story many times about his minimal relationship with his father, but it was not an involved topic of conversation simply a point in time and a small part of his history that he shared with me. His mother was a tough hard-working independent Scottish woman with traditional values but very unforgiving. She was a disciplinarian and dominant in nature despite her small stature, true of most Scottish women of her generation. I would guess I know my father's upbringing was always a challenge but despite this, he was adamant to seek independence as soon as possible. He always stated that school was not his forte, but he fell easily into sport and in his teens, he became the county triple jump champion verging on Olympic team selection, until he fell out with his coach and was dropped for any possible trials and selection. How different things might have been had he been given the opportunity.

He turned to college in the town of Northampton "the home of shoes", to study leather technology, rising rapidly through the ranks and passing every exam and qualification needed to progress at each level. To this day I do not know what steered him on this path, a mixture of something to do or any excuse to remove himself from the harshness of home and the single parent upbringing. As the years progressed, he found employment with two global films BASF and Rohm & Hass - probably the two largest chemical companies of the 70's with specific remits for leather production and chemical production for the tanning process. This led to overseas employment in various global locations from Latin and Central America to Europe and then to Mexico City and hence my arrival in this world.

Work was the very driver for my father and still is at the age of 74. Still self-employed working a nine-to-five day, albeit in a completely different sector. He was relentless in climbing the corporate ladder and taking home the bacon. First class worldwide travel, relocation expenses and homes in each country he worked were all provided for. There was nothing he could not achieve. Granted that times were quite different back then, but he never failed to put in the graft to provide the best for us and he did on every level. Despite the obvious material rewards and trappings of success, my mother was not fond of being so far away from family in this distant part of the world. The culture, the language, and the frequent earthquakes, that on occasions had my mother diving under the table with me in her arms to protect me from the house collapsing on top of us. These were all very strange and uncomfortable surroundings. It was a far cry from the rural home of Northamptonshire. In 1976, my folks came back to the UK and during this time my brother made his appearance in the world.

My mother was raised in Northampton with her older sister to working class parents who were not wealthy by any stretch but had enough and managed to get through. My grandmother was part of the land girls during the war, as were many grandparents during this time so cohesiveness and solidarity to support others in adversity was order of the day. My maternal grandmother was from London's east end and had a down to earth upbringing where family togetherness and structure was deemed far more important than the trappings of success unless you were in the underworld. Well, there was not much wealth and success during these times in any case but helping and supporting those in the community was valued part of life.

My mother had a safe and happy upbringing and was part of the typical family unit. Both her parents remained together for the duration of their lives despite the obvious strains I can now recall as a child when I spent time with my grandparents. My mother was the typical and socially accepted housewife and stay at home mum with two kids to raise. Never career focused but educated to a good level in secretarial skills she mainly held roles within the office PA environment. When returning from Mexico my father was posted to Croydon, the UK head office, and so he decided to buy a house down south rather than in his hometown of Northampton due to the commute. We settled in a small town called Forest Row in East Sussex. A grand house on a new estate that was ground-breaking in those days in terms of its design. (Grand Designs Kevin McLeod style house springs to mind). I can say without doubt probably one of the coolest houses available at the time. Futuristic by design, huge slanting copper roof and windows in the split-level lounge that were like shop fronts overlooking the fields. A very retro-inspired, yet futuristic house by design that I was fortunate to live in. It was a very affluent part of the country and still is today.

Our family settled and we were living the typical dream. It took blood, sweat and tears on all levels by both my parents in various parts of the world and challenges they faced but they had made it. My father must have felt so proud to have achieved this, despite his modest and hard upbringing and I guess much of his happiness was an element of proving his mother wrong on some level and being the father to us that he never had. For this I will always be grateful. Job security was never an issue as it is today. He had stable and dependable employment and he was at the top of his game in the corporate world.

Money was good, life was good, and we had it all. As kids we had great stability and routine in family life as well as great holidays abroad and the best toys for Christmas. We were extremely fortunate to have the material abundance during this time, even my dad's cars were a rare sight. A bright orange three litre Ford Capri parked on the driveway, harping back to era of the TV drama the Professionals. A great car until he wrapped it round a lamp post on the hill into the estate one winter. His driving hasn't got any better to this day and is still much source of amusement amongst the family.

CHAPTER 2

CHILDHOOD

This, I guess, is where most of what I now know about who I am came from, these formative years as a child. Most of you will have read that from birth to the age of seven or ten years of age our experiences shape who we are on a subconscious level. This is your programming. You begin to form understandings about right and wrong, what your boundaries are, you learn your parent's behaviours and take on board their characteristics.

Your parents, by default, will have subconsciously raised you akin to how they experienced childhood. There is also a belief that they try not to raise you in a way they experienced their own childhood, by overcompensating in some ways to avoid their recollection of their pains and what it would put you through as a child. Now for us, that meant that my dad was very controlling, dominant sometimes, angry with us and came down hard on us when we were up to no good or being naughty. A good smack, a raised voice and told to go to our room was probably the harshest form of punishment. It was delivered in a manner that scared the shit out of both me and my brother, and we soon learned how to keep in line or meet his expectations.

My dad was only repeating how his mother had handled his wayward behaviour on some level. On some occasions my mother would step in and shelter us from the wrath of my dad's rage. At no point can I recall any harsh abuse to us, but I guess by today's health and safety mad world it would have been frowned upon to some extent. It was just my father's way of teaching us the traditional and hereditary values of respect and appreciation for elders, which I guess stems from many ancestral timelines, from generational and social

7

cycles. Repeating with each generation adapting to the way of the world at the time and place, based on social acceptance, morals and ethical beliefs.

These patterns of behaviour are passed down from generation to generation. Everyone walking this earth is programmed this way, with the obvious cultural and religious factors taken on board depending on your ethic group and place in the world. But we are all programmed and sadly no one is exempt from this.

My mum told me in recent conversations that I was quite jealous of my brother in our younger years and as such, we would often fight and wind each other up. It is, again, a family programme mirrored throughout the years where sibling rivalry is seen and experienced as we fight for attention from our care givers. Such was my mum's frustration and desperation at times that she felt my dad's intervention was often required to stop the drama and put us in our place. I am sure that this is the same story for many children who had petty squabbles over toys, friends, life choices right and wrongs. We have all been there, I am sure. Despite my accepted and believed way of life, we were grounded, sensible, did not take risks and were generally well-balanced kids. What I take from this now is the fact that we were somewhat controlled by our parents and to some degree, were never able to fully express who we were as kids and I believe the same could be said for most of the people reading this narrative.

Our exuberance and enthusiasm as kids was tempered, and rarely encouraged. We were told to be quiet, dress a certain way, behave a certain way because of social acceptance and the morals of the time. Now I am not advocating this is right or wrong, just making an observation about a practice that has evolved over time.

The opposite could be said of those kids whose parents let their kids be free to be who they are with little or no control or smothering by doting parents. We all know those kids at school who were always pushing the boundaries and acting up, and you always saw their parents walking into school to have a meeting with the headmaster following an event at school, chances are a week later, they were doing the same thing again it is like their parents couldn't do anything with them or chose to ignore the problems.

These are very opposing ways of child reading practices, but they both have damaging subconscious implications for people later in life and has been clearly documented over the years of study.

From the age of about six or seven I had one close friend who lived in the house opposite us, the same age as me but from a quite different background and parental structure. I always remember going round to his house and there was never a positive vibe in the house. He had an older sister who was never around, his dad worked away a lot and his mum - well I'm not sure what she did or what she was about, but she was very rarely at home. She was a nice lady and was always polite and friendly but never engaged in conversation or made time for us kids. She was very distant and would always be doing her own thing. Looking back now, I cannot recall many occasions where our parents involved themselves with our friends at all except for the obligatory yearly birthday party and school events. Perhaps they did and I was not conscious of it, too busy messing about I guess, to pay any significant attention to my surroundings at that age.

Now, I could go on about all my childhood exploits growing up but to be honest they are probably no different to yours. The friends, the scrapes we got into, the many first experiences as I made my way in the world. One thing I do recall from childhood that was traumatic for me that only just came to light during the last twelve months and a period of deep reflection and meditation, was the effect on my subconscious mind of a condition I had which to this day baffles me and I guess my parents. From as early as I can remember until I was about fourteen, I was a serial "bed wetter'. I recall the rubber sheets, the alarms, the endless medications, and drugs and waking up in the night to change the sheets and pyjamas once or twice a night. The endless doctors' appointments etc. to try different things, even hypnosis in my early teens.

This condition without doubt had the most profound subconscious effect on me, which at the time I accepted as part of normal day life and a condition that would live with for the rest of my life. My parents, well mum mainly, tried everything and exhausted all avenues to try and resolve this issue for me and I cannot express how much her efforts meant to me at the time. I do not recall ever having a diagnosis or reason for this condition, but I can only assume it came about because of some trauma which affected me on some level. Was that in the womb or at birth with my mum having the C section to bring me into the world, or did I suffer because of the chord round my neck? I guess I will never know. Or was it as result of being devoid of physical touch from my mum in the first 48 hrs of my new life.

To say this condition obviously affected my ability to be a normal child would be an understatement in some regards. Sleepovers were never a thing for me and holidays and trips away with parents were always a source of constant worry and anxiety for me. It is only now that I realise just how much I was missing out on because of this issue. As a result, I became quite insular and independent, not spending much time close to anyone. I guess I was a fearful avoidant. Constantly fearful of being close to people in case I smelt of urine! We have all been in that queue in the shops standing next to someone who clearly does, and it is not a nice experience. Although I washed every day, I guess subconsciously my mind must have made this judgement about it whether that was real or perceived. Even if I did smell, I am sure nobody would have felt open enough to tell me as a child for fear of upsetting me. I was conscious of my condition but tried in vain not to let it affect me negatively. My parents were certainly there to have my back at any given moment should something ever become an issue. I cannot help now, thinking back, just how limiting this was for me and just how much it held me back as a person, on all levels. Mentally and subconsciously, I was not normal, I was not like the other kids. As I sit here and write this, I wonder how many other kids had their issues back then that they too were hiding from the world or whose parents sheltered them from opening up about, for fear of feeling less than, or worthy of acceptance and love? I guess our parents just want us to be as normal as possible to fit in with the social norm.

When I was nine or ten, my dad found another job in Northamptonshire and so we moved lock, stock, and barrel back to their home turf after all those years of travelling around. It was my mum's influence I guess, that persuaded my dad to return to his hometown and perhaps my dad was also feeling a pull to return to roots after having been all over the place for so many years and never really settling. I guess my mum was missing her parents also, with two growing kids to manage she felt a move would allow us to spend more time with our grandparents as we all do at some stage.

We moved to a small hamlet in Northamptonshire with a population of about two hundred at the time, and into a large newly renovated coach house that was huge in comparison to where we had just moved from but equally grand. This was to be my last family home where I would live for the rest of my childhood into my mid 20's. We had to find new friends, attend a new school, and start over again. The transition was relatively easy for both me and my brother and we adapted to the new way of life. We were out in the countryside far from urban civilization or that is how it felt. But what opened for us was a new way of life and experiences. My new school was in the next village and I quickly settled in and made some new friends, one of whom was also new to the area and had moved down from Yorkshire with his family. We became close friends and had a similar outlook on things. We were both finding the experience challenging.

It was suggested to me, to join the local cub scout group, as many boys of my age did, to learn new things and have a wider circle of friends, and much fun was experienced doing all the things cub scouts do. It was a great time for me, and I quickly acquired two sleeves of badges for new skills learnt and mastered. Outdoor pursuits were plentiful, and I made good use of these skills when playing in the countryside near to our new home. We spent hours in the woods, fields and farmlands that surrounded the village, and much time was spent on the second world war air force base that was just outside the village. We explored derelict bomb shelters and old mess halls that littered the landscape for miles, always in search of some old war relics. Bits of old aeroplanes and bullet casings were commonly found.

My bedwetting condition was still very much a part of my life, but as I was getting older it was becoming more manageable. However, I became more anxious as I progressed in life and started to head towards my early teens. I do recall going on one school trip, as I guess my mum wanted me not to miss out on the experience, The fear surrounding that trip and about my condition was so much for me to deal with and every night, I would lay awake fearful of falling asleep in case I wet the bed in front of my friends. Unfortunately, it happened on a few nights and having lived with this most of my childhood I was able to hide this embarrassment from the others who were in the same room as me. The teachers were aware of my issues and were incredibly supportive and made sure I was OK.

I cannot recall much of the trip as most of the time I was so anxious and in fear. I guess part of me was angry at my parents for making me go, but I also see that had I not gone, things would have been less rewarding for me in facing these issues head on. At some point I would need to face these fears and deal with it myself as it was pretty much down to me now. The trip did force me to step up a little and face this head on and I guess I can be thankful for the experience, but the years of anxiety and worry were the formative part of my subconscious programming because of this condition.

By the age of fourteen, my condition stopped one night and was never part of my life again which was a relief for sure, but the years of self-loathing and doubt were clearly a part of who I had become. A feeling of being less than was always part of my mindset as a direct result of this experience, but something I was not conscious of until recently, and certainly unaware of the subconscious impact that has ruled over me for the last forty-seven years.

The only positive memory I have of the trip, is one sheer determination and resilience by me and my friend. We were herded into the minibus and taken down to a beach in Christchurch on the south coast. It was a beachcombing, rock pool learning kind of day and off we went, clipboards in hand to record our finds. My friend and I must have walked the entire length of the beach from one end to the other, in an attempt to get away from the rest of the school. We came to the end of the beach and sat messing about waiting for the others to catch up. Once caught up we all came together with the teaching staff for an update on the morning's events.

After lunch we were allowed some time to ourselves while the teachers watched over the group as we went exploring once again. We were herded up after an hour and told to start heading back to the minibus. At this point my friend suggested we run back to the bus, again beating the crowd. Now my friend was a chronic asthmatic and spent pretty much of the morning sucking on his inhaler and taking a cocktail of drugs, such was his limiting condition. We set off jogging down the beach with teachers shouting at us not to go too far ahead! We ignored them completely as we set off at pace. Now to this day, I do not know how long the beach was but for us it felt like at least two miles in length if not more. Both of us ran the entire length of this beach without stopping at all and we reached the minibus in what seemed like days ahead of the others.

We sat and waited again for the others to catch up. Not once did my friend reach for his inhaler or complain about his condition and he was smiling from ear to ear at what he had just achieved. We both felt a sense of enormous joy at our achievement, as we watched from a distance the others that were trying to emulate our feats without much success, stopping every few hundred yards and starting up again. We both laughed as they were unable to match our achievement.

In that moment both of us felt that despite our own personal issues we were unstoppable. We both felt on top and we both knew our worth, and it gave us a sense of just how capable we were as humans to overcome adversity. We felt that nothing is impossible if we put our minds to it and–let go of the fears and learn to accept things in the moment.

Now in my early teens, the move to secondary school was another milestone in my evolution. Despite not going to church and living or practising a strong Christian upbringing, I managed to get into the local Church of England School - partly down to the fact my father pulled a few strings with the local vicar, who we often saw, as our house was next to the village church. This did not go down well with some other parents in the village, but my father's attitude I guess was "who gives a shit about them anyway". His approach to the whole situation was remarkably like when the Jehovah's witness door knockers came to your house to try and engage in polite conversation on a Sunday morning. "Oh, just fuck off", he would tell them - never one to shy away from a direct approach.

Secondary school for me was an OK experience. It was a great school in the town near to where we lived, and out of all the local schools this was the preferred choice for parents and hence the religious connotations for acceptance into it. I had friends from junior school, from the village and cub scouts all at my new school, so I was not isolated in this regard. I had a ridiculously small circle of close friends and I guess my friends equally stayed under the radar to some extent too.

We were the kind of small friendship group that attracted the idiots and the bullies of the school in our year group and were quite often the cause of much ridicule and bullying by others, A source of fun and amusement that often led to items of clothing being ripped or torn or stuff being broken. Then having to go home to our parents, lying about what had cause the ripped coats, the split new school trousers or broken rucksacks. At no time were there any proper fights or physical altercations, it was more the threat of after school of when we left the safety of the grounds of the school that things took a turn for the worst and sometimes got a big ugly.

I was not the academic type in the slightest, a bit like the old man, and struggled with all the important lessons like Maths and English and to this day would struggle doing even the basics of Maths like percentages, fractions etc, and even writing this book would be considered well beyond my comprehension of English grammar and writing abilities. My forte was art and the creative lessons like woodwork, metal work and so on.

I guess my creativity came from being isolated as a child by my own choice and always finding something to do by myself, either building a den, drawing, playing with Lego or just making things, which I did all the time. I have always had a curious and creative mind and have always been eager to explore things in detail. Like so many others I was more stimulated on the visual plain rather than by text or words. Pictures and images were always more interesting to me and using my hands to create. I have always been good with my hands and I am a very capable and practical person.

Most lunchtimes you would find me in the art room with my best friend catching up on lessons or painting something, partly because that is what we loved doing and it kept us away from the bullies of the school. Now, obviously aside from general aspects of school lessons, scrapes and being accepted, the other area of interest was girls. Yes, this is when most of us find an interest in the opposite sex.

Group peer pressure and acceptance was part of this experience. I guess my first experience with a girl was around thirteen years of age at the school disco, when I had the typical snog in a dark corner of the hall with a girl in my form group. Snogging was a way to be accepted within the social group back then. I don't think much has changed in all these years, it seems to be a right of passage as people hit their mid-teens and very much a part of growing up.

CHAPTER 3

SEXUAL DISCOVERY

Now, for me this topic is relatively straightforward. I am a straight heterosexual male, always have been and always will be. Again, raised with the programme and belief that as a man I should only interested in women or the fairer sex, such was my stereotypical upbringing that had taught me. I have no desire to alter, change or be anything other than a straight heterosexual male.

This is for me, perhaps is where my understanding of acceptance, emotions, and feelings of what I thought love is stems from, and why I was never able to fully explore and realise a deep unconditional love for someone else in the way I see it now. Like I said in the beginning, I have no experiences of sexual abuse, part taken in or done anything in a sexual way to harm others. My experiences I guess, will account for most people reading this narrative and be no different to what most people experience with sexual freedoms and growing up as kids.

My first ever sexual experience was with my best friend at the age of eight or nine. Yes, a boy we were both boys and learning and finding out about our bodies at that time as kids do. I do not think I am any different to anyone out there on this. I do recall around this age whilst playing hide and seek in my home I hid under my parents' bed. I stumbled across my father's collection of adult magazines. You know the sort, Playboy Mayfair all early 80 stuff and quite tame by today's material. Obviously back then it was still taboo to some extent and liberal attitudes were still muted in this seedy underworld of society, but my curiosity got the better of me and I started to flick through the pages.

I recall my feelings of arousal growing as you would expect and that my body was changing, my heart racing and feeling all funny and I started to have my first erection. As my brother came up the stairs a quickly put my find away and pretend nothing had happened. After what seemed a few minutes, my brother found me, and the game was up, quite literally. I recall going to bed that night with an urge to revisit those magazines again to see if the feelings I felt would return bearing in mind this was all new to me and my first real experience of feeling sexually aroused.

A few days later I plucked up the courage to return to the stash under the bed and took one of the magazines into the bathroom for a longer look, locking the door behind me I began to turn the pages and take in all that I was seeing. It was the same experience as before, and within minutes I began playing with myself. It was the best feeling in the world to me. Even to this day I can recall the images in my mind such was the vivid potency of this situation on such a young mind. I guess many men reading this can relate to this first experience of arousal by whatever means, and I am sure women who read their first erotic novel will also have a similar experience. Having a conversation with my best friend he too confirms the same experience and the discovery of his dad's stash. I guess it was a sign of the times.

The shame and guilt of my actions I guess never really affected me, as the feelings of euphoria far outweighed any negative emotions and feelings. What was I doing that was so wrong? I was not stealing, I was not hurting anyone, no one knew, it was just me. How could this be wrong, and it felt ok? If it was OK for my dad then it must be OK for me too? This pattern of behaviour continued for a number of weeks until one day the magazines vanished. I can only assume the game was up, either my parents knew or suspected something was wrong, but I never knew what happened, as I guess any topic of conversation on this matter was deemed too inappropriate for a child of my age.

Needless to say, my quest to explore this newfound excitement spurred on my desires even more. Before long I was talking to my best friend about it and on a few occasions, we played with each other. As friends having both discovered these feelings of arousal, we enlisted another friend, who was female, into our games and fun was had by all. Now this was all very innocent and a part of our growing up and everyone reading this will have a similar story or experience for that I am certain. For some it will be a pleasurable memory, for others a horrific experience that have suffered sexual abuse or been ill-treated in this way. For those that have had a bad experience, I am deeply sorry for your pain and suffering that you did not deserve. For me, this experience was a choice and for someone who felt unloved, alone, and unable to get close to people because of my medical condition, it was my go-to place to feel that love and emotional acceptance for myself, and to feel accepted by others too or to feel normal. I saw no wrong in what I was doing nor did I feel it was wrong. The fact that my first experience of sexual arousal in the physical sense was with another boy only opened my curiosity to this experience and what sexuality meant to me as a child.

My second sexual experience was with a girl in the village where I grew up in my teens. She was probably my ultimate desire as a teenager growing up. Tall, leggy, blonde, with a stunning figure who

21

always smelt divine - she was the whole package. We spent pretty much every day together as close friends for years and although we never became sexually involved with each other as girlfriend and boyfriend there were many times, we enjoyed kissing and touching each other physically. I used to spend hours in her bedroom watching her get ready to go out on dates and she would try different outfits on and ask me which one I thought looked the best. I would just sit there in a permanent state of teenage arousal. The feelings of wanting to be with her in a sexual way and not being able to, I guess formed my subconscious attachment to women. She used to let me massage her sometimes and that would be as close as I ever got.

I knew at this point in my life that I was only interested in women she had sealed that fate for me. I guess my years growing up with her, I felt deep emotional and sexual connection more than most to the female sex. She was my best friend and confidante for many years throughout my teenage years, a bond and attachment on the subconscious mind that was hard to shake off. Not that I ever wanted to, as I was perhaps one of the only boys who had such a friend at the time and was often quizzed about my interactions with her by curious male friends.

My need and desire to explore these emotions of sexuality and my intimate feelings always got the better of me and when faced with the dilemma of not being with someone on an intimate level, I guess I struggled emotionally to connect with people I felt a loving connection with. My use of online interactions in my later years was just a way to deal with these emotions and was my safe place. I was never judged, I was never embarrassed, I was never in fear of rejection or being accepted and it was my way of making me happy when I felt unloved or

22

uncared for by someone. I realised that regular masturbation was not a bad thing and quite a healthy thing. But I understand and accept it is not something most would admit to openly.

Now 18, and considered an adult, I was working in a Hotel part time as a waiter and the hotel was run by a small Bavarian businessman "mini-Hitler" as he was affectionately named by the staff. For me this was a great time in my life. I worked all hours I could such was the buzz of hotel life, night after night of parties and celebrations and all the shenanigans' people got up to. There are many stories I could share, and things witnessed and was privy too, but you get the picture.

"Mini Hitler" arranged for some women from his hometown to come over and work in the hotel for a season, sort of like an exchange trip but for working staff. I instantly had become very fond of a young lady from this trio of ladies from another world. She was your stereotypical blonde German lady tall, elegant softly spoken, lovely eyes and figure to die for, a young Claudia Schiffer if you will. We often took breaks together as we chatted and became friends. Feelings for each other developed over time and I plucked up the courage to invite her out on a date. To my surprise she agreed, and things only developed from there.

We spent most evenings after work back in her room in a separate staff block in the hotel car park. We would listen to music, talk and eventually get more intimate with each other as our relationship evolved. I would often be seen by the night porter driving home in the early hours of the morning screeching out of the carpark trying to slip away. I was hoping that she would be my first true fully blown sexual relationship. I prayed and hoped that I would finally know what it felt like to have sex with a woman.

It was nearing Christmas and she was feeling a little sad not being back home with family, so I invited her to my home for a few days whilst my parents were away. We had our own little Christmas celebration, exchanged gifts, and settled into a few days of solitude just the two of us. We spent every hour together romantically snuggled up getting closer and closer to each other. Was this the time I was going to finally feel what it was like to have sex with a woman for the first time? Not only that, but she was from another country and different class of woman altogether which made the attraction and desire for this experience more exhilarating than most, I felt on top of the world.

We decided to head to bed early, and my nerves were shot! I was shaking at the very thought of seeing this woman naked in front of me let alone the act of having sex with her. We passionately kissed and started to undress each other, each taking it in turns to remove an item of each other's clothing. Within minutes she was standing in front of me naked. Now the sheer sight of this woman in clothes would bring most men to the knees but seeing her naked was far too much for me to deal with. My friends had often teased me about my new German friend saying that she would have hairy armpits and leg stubble not to mention down below. They were right! How did they know.

This was a far cry from what thought I knew and my expectations. Despite the obvious shock on my part the sheer sight of this woman naked in front of me sprouting the Black Forest from every crevasse I was not going to be deterred one bit. I had come this far I was not going to throw in the towel just yet. We enjoyed playing with each other kissing and touching each other but sadly the intensity of this woman and her touch made sure that I was not in a fit state to have sex if you catch my drift, it was over before it could begin. She was very loving and generous and not at all critical of my dismal performance at the time, which made the shame even more frustrating for me to deal with. We got into bed and spent the night in each other's arms until the morning when I gave her a lift back to the hotel.

Despite my continued efforts to pursue this woman, it was clear that my attempts were not fully appreciated, and she decided that she no longer wanted to see me. Having to still work with her daily was torture, she would often pass a smile at me and a caring glance but any dream I had of having sex with her was now a distant dream, I had my chance and blew it. A few months later she was posted back home and to this day never heard from her again. It was one of those experiences you never forget and never forgive yourself for.

Shortly after her departure I managed to secure a place at Birmingham College of Food, Tourism and Creative Studies and was accepted on to the HND course studying Hotel and Catering and Institutional Management. My time in school was not rewarding and so I was fortunate to obtain a place and felt much excitement to be doing something I was already passionate about having worked for "Mini-Hitler" - the Bavarian bulldog! This was a chance for me to make something of myself and forge a career. I recall driving to Northampton Train station and catching the train to Birmingham for enrolment day. It was a huge step for me, a reserved shy country lad, stepping into city life and mixing with a whole new world of people from different cultures and ethnicities.

I spent the day registering for my course and whilst outside minding my own business made friends with a guy also on his own. He was to be my friend throughout my college years. He was a big fella and reminded me of the actor John Goodman who played Roseanne's husband in the American sitcom of the same name. A gentle giant who I was pleased to be friends within this new world of mine. He was kind of a protection for me such was his stature and I felt safe with him around.

The first year of College went well. I passed all my exams and pretty much excelled in all areas such was my passion for this subject, a far cry from my school years. I do regret not living in Birmingham during these years and as such, probably missed out on many things and experiences, but I guess my subconscious mind and ego kept me safe by commuting everyday rather than stepping out by myself in the fullest of the context. The comfort of home was all too familiar and had been my safe haven during much of my childhood and associated health conditions, which held me back and it was still doing it now even years later. During this time, I started to work for a new hotel chain in my hometown in the evenings and weekends, and so pretty much every hour of my life was consumed in this field of work and learning. Now whilst the choice of women and possible dates was far greater at college, I decided not to forge any meaningful sexual relationships with women at college preferring the blonde in the reception at the new place of work.

My subconscious mind was playing out an old pattern again from past experiences. Blonde, tall, blue eyes and amazing body. Here we go again! She was not German but certainly had that Nordic look about her, despite being local and British she too, was a feast for the eyes. Again, the same pattern repeated itself, regular lunch breaks timed to coincide with hers meant we formed a friendship and started to flirt with each other. Now, older and wiser and with some experience under my belt I was determined to make this experience count. Within a few short months I was round her house after work in her bedroom, ripping each other's clothes off and without any hesitation committing fully to the task ahead. We had sex and it was as good as I had dreamed it would be. I had finally made it!

What ensued was four months of complete lust driven experiences between us at every opportunity we could find. Having lost my virginity to this woman I guess I wanted to experience everything that I had previously thought about and dreamed about up to this point, and she did not disappoint. As soon as our relationship had started, it ended when the new guy from the gym took an interest in her and behind my back, they slept together at a party, which I only found out about through a waitress I was working with one night. To be honest I was not that concerned or worried, more relieved that I had done the deed and it was with her. I had joined that elusive club and felt I had grown up, so to speak. I had a newfound confidence and appreciation for what I thought love was.

Back at college for my second year, should have been industrial placement time where we headed off to some swanky hotel and spent a year in industry. Most of my friends secured hotels overseas but sadly I was unable to locate a hotel and decided to stay behind and complete my second-year study whilst friends were out on placement. It was a good year and with a new friend in tow, a guy called Staci (yes, a girl's name), a Hispanic chap who I connected with straight away as I was born in Mexico, so I felt we had a connection of sorts and an automatic right to be his side kick such was the Latino connection. The reality of the Latino connection in the real context was as far apart as you could imagine to be honest, but we felt connected all the same.

This second year was a major experience and life lesson. None of my new friends were white, and I was immersed into friend groups of black African, Asian, and Indian cultures. I was the only white kid on the block. I also found out that Staci was the UK's leading Thai kickboxing champion with national acclaim and so felt totally at ease with my new surroundings despite being the only "whitey" in the group. Most of the tall, athletic, 6 ft, Stormzy, Snoop Dog and Fifty Cent lookalikes all built like brick shit houses seemed to look up to Staci in a way and so I never felt an air of threat from any of these guys, as I knew Staci would kick their ass, despite being no taller than me, had they attempted any racial tensions with me.

Many good times I had with my newfound friends, too many to list here, but it was a time I will be forever grateful for, not at least it gave me an appreciation for other ethnic groups and cultures, something I think everyone should be open to experience rather than the stereotypical views we hold because of events portrayed in the media. I guess being amongst women of different ethnic groups was of an interest to me on a sexual level, but there was still at this time some stigma and racial prejudices that I guess prevented my mind from allowing me to take a physical step in this direction. There was a fear attached to dating a woman of colour or different race such was the way I was raised and the social conditioning around this life choice. I was attracted deeply to their caring and supportive nature, as much of the black and afro Caribbean heritage is deeply religious and faith-based roots and that was clear to me as I witnessed groups of these women embraced in a community vibe around the college. They were always very welcoming and warm people which will always be remembered.

CHAPTER 4

STEPPING OUT ON MY OWN

With my second year at college having been completed earlier than expected and blazing through my exams, I was now ready to take my year out on placement. I managed to secure a slot at one of the other hotels within the chain I was already working for down on the south coast. It was a far cry from my preferred placement of Bermuda, for which I had family connections so thought It would be a breeze to get in. Sadly, the requirements and paperwork needed, not to mention my available income and bank balance at the time made this an impossibility during the application process.

I set off to Fareham, in my new car my father had bought for me - a Mk 1 Golf silver GLS (Germany's finest of which I already had an appreciation for) to a town between Portsmouth and Southampton called Fareham, where the hotel was situated just off the M27. I settled into the staff house and began my life away from home. The house was a big Victorian villa style house in the main town and was sparsely furnished but it was home for the next year. I felt confident and self-assured in my new venture and quickly found my feet making yet more new friends and colleagues within the hotel. I went through each department over the coming months learning everything inside out.

My sexual experiences were rudely awakened and somewhat re-ignited when I joined the ladies in Housekeeping for a month. This was a real baptism of fire. I do not mind saying I was knackered at the end of each day. These women who do this job deserve a medal. The work is at a fast pace and backbreaking. Each shift I was paired with a different woman from the housekeeping team and assisted her to do the rounds. Normally 25 to 30 rooms each day. After a week I was placed with one lady for a whole week much to my surprise. She was an older woman who was extremely slender and extremely attractive always impeccably turned out and made up every shift.

Of all the women she was stunning, and not the kind you would think would be doing this kind of work. I make no judgements, but it just seemed odd. She showed me the ropes and we got to work on her round. After about five rooms into the shift on the second day, the conversation between us became very flirtatious and occasionally overstepped the professional work boundary line if you like. Now as a man of the world or so I thought, I was accepting of it and quite enjoyed the banter with her. There were sexual connotations and innuendos flying everywhere. I did pause for a moment and question where this was heading, and I did have to gather my thoughts. I was on my college placement and the thought of doing something stupid and jeopardizing my whole future rushed through my mind. I decided to act professional and carry on with the job in hand such was my reputation and desire to succeed academically at something and make my parents proud.

Fifteen rooms in and halfway through the shift we broke for lunch. Entering the staff canteen, I chose to sit with some other friends from the hotel but noticed my housekeeping chaperone staring and making suggestive comments towards me as I tried to eat lunch. On returning to work with her we started in the next room. As I was making the bed and was bending over to see to the hospital corners, and she decided to grab my arse. I stood up in a blind panic and she was standing right

31

in front of me, face to face smiling and with her uniform strategically unbuttoned. Looking me dead in the eye she said she "I want you" as she leaned forward and kissed me passionately. I thought I knew what a kiss was, but clearly not! This was on a different level.

As tempted as I was by her advances, I knew there was a time and a place, and this was neither. I tempered my urges towards her and said I could not get involved. She was a married woman with young kids, and I knew my position was a risk. We carried on and finished the shift and I went back to the staff house to contemplate what had happened. I was obviously deeply attracted by the thought of having a sexual encounter with a much older woman of her calibre, but I just knew it was wrong on every level. I was relaxing in my room and the doorbell rang. As I was the only one in the house, I went to open the door only to be greeted by my housekeeping friend who was all dressed up and looking stunning. I was completely surprised and out of my depth when she asked "do you want to go out for a drink". I had to decline her offer as some of my colleagues came up the driveway from having been at work and spotted who she was. I said sorry and closed the door and went back to my room.

A few moments later my work colleagues were entering my room like the Spanish inquisition asking me all sorts of questions about my doorstep visitor. I denied all acknowledgement of what they were suggesting. I recall waking up the next morning dreading the day working with her. I arrived at work to start my day and there she was waiting for me. What preceded was her explaining to me that she was not getting any attention from her husband and she needed some fun. She also proceeded to tell me she was an ex-glamour model and missed her work and wanted to live out her passionate youthful days again and could not understand why her advances were being rejected by me. I explained my situation to her, and she reluctantly accepted my position. We remained professional and civil with each other until the end of that week. I couldn't wait for my next departmental assignment and hopefully with less distractions or compromising circumstances to deal with.

I was posted to the restaurant until the end of the festive holidays and whilst working in the restaurant we had some seasonal staff join the team. One woman came into work and I was instantly attracted to her. My passions and desires had obviously been stirred by the lustful lady from housekeeping, but this woman was of my age, single and simply stunning. She was out of my league and pretty much every other hot-blooded male in the hotel was trying it on with her, from the chef to the porter to the hotel manager from what the rumours had been suggesting, so sometimes you just got to know when to quit.

After the new year celebrations had died down and the hotel returned to some normal level of activity, I decided to return home for my 21st Birthday. I had been away from home for some months and knew I had to get back for this celebration. A chance to celebrate with old friends and of course family. I packed my car up and headed home on the three-hour drive. During my time in Fareham, my car had been in and out of the garage multiple times for this and that and was worse than useless at this point. Despite endless trips to the garage and hundreds of pounds spent trying to keep me mobile I was unsure if the German wonder would get me home at all. I set off and it drove without fault all the way back home until about five miles from home when the vorsprung durch technic decided to die on its arse.

I called my dad who came to the rescue as he had done with all the garage bills. Having never towed anything before he decided to bump me all the way home five miles by shoving me from behind with his car bumper. With whiplash and head injuries, we made it back home an hour later than expected and we went inside.

As I walked through the front door, I could sense that things were not right. There was a tense and cold atmosphere in the house, and the old man looked like he had been through hell and back. Despite his brave front I knew something was amiss and asked him what was wrong. He said, "I will tell you all about it tomorrow", I said, "where's mum?" and he said" in bed". As strange as I thought it was that my mum was not there to greet me, I too hit the sack as it was nearing eleven in the evening and I was knackered. I woke in the morning early which was unusual for me when on holiday and went to get a cup of tea. Mum was in the kitchen pottering around and I could see she was also not a hundred percent herself. I asked her if everything was alright and as parents do, she said "fine". We hugged and she walked out of the kitchen as I made my cuppa. As I stood pondering the reason for the atmosphere my dad popped in and I again asked if everything was OK. He then spent the best part of 10 minutes explaining that he and mum were not getting on and that he felt they were about to get a divorce.

I was in complete shock and speechless as he offered his heart out in front of me, part sadness, part rage was clearly visible on his face. He left the kitchen assuring me that everything would be fine. When I left six months ago, all was fine in my eyes and I had come home to this! I gathered my thoughts and went in search of my mum who clearly was struggling to hold herself together and hence her reluctance to be near me in any capacity. I found her sitting in the lounge and as I sat down, I asked her what was going on. She tried in to show no emotions, but it was written all over her face too, as it was my dad, they were equally in a similar place. I tried to get her to tell me what was going on when my dad came in and told my mum to tell me what was going on.

What ensued from that moment on was at least three hours of fighting, shouting door slamming tears, rage, upset and friction between my parents. With me a silent witness to the events that were unfolding in front of me, not less than twenty-four hours before my 21st birthday. My Mum decided it was time to leave and did so with vigour and haste taking a small suitcase of clothes and my dad shouting to her "if you walk out that door don't ever come back"! She never did!

There I was in the kitchen with my dad crying his eyes out, devastated, and heartbroken by the culmination of events that had transpired in the six months I was away from home. I had only ever seen my dad cry once before and that was when his mother died. I recall playing a football match one morning as he wandered across the playing field, sobbing, and embracing my mum on the touchline. A memory etched in my mind. For the second time in twenty-one years, I saw before me a man who I looked up to in so many ways completely broken, vulnerable and empty. Seeing such a strong man reduced to tears, for me was a shock as I was under the social understanding and belief that men do not show emotions or vulnerability, so this was new to me. We embraced each other in the kitchen as we both sobbed. A moment I will never forget and for the first time I felt a connection to my father from an emotional standpoint. He gathered himself together quickly and assured me everything would be ok.

After an hour or so of reflection and me also in a state of shock, we sat in the lounge and he started to tell me everything that had been going on. I sat in complete disbelief in what I was hearing but he was sincere, genuine and I had no reason not to accept the validity of what he was telling me. The tone of voice and his posture said it all. My dad has always been an honest man to my knowledge and hated any form of injustice toward others.

For me this was a trauma I was not ready to experience or expected and I guess anyone who has been through a parental separation or divorce will know just how profound and traumatic these experiences are. Sure, we move on in time and we get past the pain and the hurt, but the subconscious mind hangs on to this information and events and when you are not expecting it fuck's you over years later in your own life. With my mind all over the place the first thing I did was reach out to my best friend, who was also away at Leeds university to tell him what was happening, we chatted for an hour or so on the phone and he said he would be there for me if I ever needed anything. It was a small comfort to me knowing someone had my back in all this.

I then went down to the village and knocked on the door of my friend who I grew up with - you know the one! who I knew would comfort me in my hour of need? She listened to me and supported me as we spoke, telling me also that she was out with her current boyfriend and saw my mum in the same pub with another man. I could not believe what I was hearing but my dad's words were all starting to tie things together nicely.

I spent most of the day with my friend as we discussed how things would develop and I really had no idea what to expect or do anymore. I gathered my thoughts and returned to my Dad who was back at work as if nothing had happened. Strange as this sounds, I don't recall where my brother was in all this and I had not seen him since I had been back. We sat down for dinner and discussed how things would change going forward. He was adamant that I finished my college course and returned to work as soon as possible. He felt it would be best for me to let him deal with the fallout in his own way. With that agreed I decided that night to fix the alternator on my German wagon and drive back to Fareham that night on the eve of my 21st Birthday.

I recall sobbing my eyes out all the way back, some three hours of emotional outpouring in the comfort and safety of the car. Arriving at the staff house and gathering my stuff out the car one of my work colleagues came over to ask what I was back so soon. He could clearly see I was a complete wreck and I told him what had happened. He gave me a hug and said do not worry it would be ok and invited me out that evening with some friends. I declined his offer saying I just wanted to get some rest. A few hours' sleep and I awoke not knowing quite where I was. The last seventy-two hours had been a bit of a blur in all honesty.

I decided to go for a walk into the town centre for some fresh air. It was about six in the evening and I walked into a local shop and bought a packet of Marlboro Red cigarettes. Now I didn't smoke, and this was a bad move! but I wanted something to calm my nerves and drink was never my biggest companion in times of need. I stood against a wall and lit up this evil stick of Armageddon and began to take a drag. Coughing and spluttering I should have stamped the bloody thing out and threw them away, but despite my body's reaction to repel this drug I chugged away like my life depended on it. I felt some light relief as I chain-smoked half the pack in about an hour.

37

I turned in for work the following morning, now in the Leisure club as my department changed following the festive season and spent most days cleaning showrooms and squash courts. Much of the time on my own pondering how my dad was coping and just what was developing back home. I lasted a few more months until I had to call my college and ask them if I could return home as my dad was clearly not coping very well. I felt obligated to return home during this time of need and solidarity. The college granted my early termination of my placement such were the circumstances and I returned home and finished the remaining stint of my placement in the local hotel where I was working part time during my first year at college.

In the few months that remained before returning home, I went on a bit of a bender, drinking and partying just to let off some steam I guess which made dealing with the fall out a little more bearable. I recall having a Friday night out in the town with few friends and we must have drunk two or three bottles of tequila between us shot after shot of the Mexican nectar. In my state of mind, I was going for it big time. Stopping via the burger van on the way back home to soak up the alcohol I remember collapsing in my room, dropping the half-eaten grease mountain covered in garlic mayo all over the floor.

I woke up in the morning, half in my bed and my face pressed against the wall, to this day I do not know whether I climbed into bed or my friends helped me into it, to make my sorry ordeal more comfortable. What I did notice was the wall was covered in vomit so was my bed and floor. My surroundings looked like a scene from a massacre. I soon realized that I was not in a good place. The realisation that I could have choked to death on my own vomit was a stark reminder, as was the pain in my head that I had gone too far in trying to deal with this situation. I spent a few days recovering from my self-inflicted ordeal and returned to work trying to behave myself for the remaining time I was there.

A few weeks before my inevitable departure it was decided by the guys in the staff house to have a little send-off party which I duly accepted. We gathered in one of the guy's rooms and started drinking and generally messing about as things go. The talk and banter ensued about football, women, and anything else that came to mind, fuelled by cans of Red Stripe as it was on offer down the local corner shop. One of the guys who was a chef at the hotel, started to roll a few joints and pass them round. Now I had smoked the" herb" as it was referred to in this part of the world a few times before and had a pleasant experience. I guess this was down to the fact I was with my closest friends with whom I trusted implicitly so I guess my mind was in a different place when I had previously indulged. My head this time was a mess, and I was with people I really had no connection with, nor did I trust, hence the experience I will share with you was not a pleasant one. Now as I was smoking every day at this point, the thought of having a few spliffs did not phase me at all. By a way of being accepted into this circle of people I puffed away with great gusto. Within about half an hour I was wasted! and made my excuses to leave the room and go and lie down for a while.

Lying on my bed I was entering into the biggest panic attack of my life. My whole body was completely numb except for my beating heart. As I lay their paralyzed, my heart was the only thing I could feel, sense, and hear such was the intensity of the feeling. If I kept moving, I was able to retain some feelings in other parts of my body and a sense of relief was restored but my heart was getting louder and louder and felt like it was going to burst out of my chest at any moment. I was in full blown paranoid drug induced panic attack. I got up out of bed, grabbed my car keys and drove to the police station in the town to summon help via what I needed which was an out of hours doctor I could see. I pulled my car up outside the police station leaving the keys in the ignition and the lights on pressed the buzzer and they let me in.

They asked what the problem was, and I said I think I am having a heart attack. They must have been wetting themselves as they called for an ambulance. I sat there being interrogated, and was repeatedly asked if I had taken anything or been given anything, with the assurances that if I had no one would get into trouble, they just wanted to make sure I was OK. Now as I sit here and recall these events, I am crying with laughter at myself at just how ridiculous I must have presented in front of these two coppers. Smelling of drugs, dying of a heart attack and having driven to the police station in my car stoned off my tits! I wish I were making this up, but I am not. I sat there being closely monitored for what seemed like hours. When a faint but recognisable sound was heard in the distance coming closer and closer, the sound of an ambulance sirens, followed by the emanating blues lights outside the police station reflecting off every surface my eyes were able to focus on. At last, I felt safe, help had arrived. I was ushered into the ambulance and connected to a heart monitor and began describing my symptoms as we sped off at high speed.

I had no idea where I was heading or how long I would be in this dream state. I rested and closed my eyes and drifted off to sleep. I awoke, having arrived at the hospital, and being helped into a wheelchair covered with a warm blanket and I was escorted by the ambulance crew, a nurse and the porter pushing me. I was wheeled through a very busy and packed A&E waiting room on a Friday night which was full of casualties in a far worse state than me. Broken bones, beaten up drunks, old and infirm all in far greater need than mine. I felt a huge sense of guilt as I was wheeled into a cubicle and assisted on the bed surrounded by three nurses checking all my vitals. I was left to sleep it off. They knew exactly what they were dealing with and probably thought what a complete arsehole for wasting valuable time and NHS care for someone stoned off his nut. To me, the experience was very real and genuine concern for my life, but as the awesome people they are they care regardless of circumstance. I have never smoked another joint to this day.

I was woken in the morning, having had the best sleep-in weeks to the doctor's morning round, a final check up with doc and I was discharged and left to find my way back home. Having been handed a brown envelope to hand to my GP. I walked free from the madness of A & E into the morning dawn chorus with no bloody idea where I was! I walked down the hill into what looked like the town centre only to be greeted on the pathway by an old lady with one of those shopping trolleys on wheels. I politely asked her where I was, to which she looked at me and must have been thinking I had fallen from outer space such was the stupidity of my question in her eyes, but perfectly rational in mine. She said, "you're in Portsmouth love" and carried on her way. I was 20 miles from home with no money, no idea where in Portsmouth I was or how I would get back home.

I saw an illuminated flashing taxi sign and headed over to see if I could get a taxi. Walking up to the caged window I spoke with the gentleman to request a taxi back to Fareham. He said, "no problem mate, that will be thirty quid". I then had to explain my predicament and despite his obvious reservations he agreed to give me a taxi on the promise I paid the driver at the other end.

We reached the staff house, and I went to open the door but had no keys! where were they? I went round the side of the house and found an open window into which I climbed through to get in to fetch my wallet to pay the driver. I entered my room and could find no sign of my wallet anywhere! Instead, I grabbed my cheque book and proceeded through the front door to pay the driver who was reluctant to accept my offer of payment, but he had no choice to be fair as I was already at my destination and now, he was out of pocket. I settled my tab and went to my room to lie down and take stock of the events of the last twenty-four hours.

I felt like my life was in free fall now and I had no parachute. Up until my parent's separation everything was fine, but now I guess everything I was attached to in the form of family, tradition, beliefs, support, guidance, and stability was shattered beyond all comprehension. I was out of control. Curious of the contents of the brown envelope that was addressed to my doctor who was three hours away in my hometown I decided to open and see for myself my diagnosis. It read "Class A drug induced panic attack. Type of drug "High grade pure cannabis".

I got ready for work as I was on the late shift at the hotel and made my way out to get in my car. Where is my car? my wallet had vanished and now the car had gone. As I stood in the driveway contemplating my next move, two of the guys at the party turned up and started to quiz me as to where I disappeared to. I did not have the balls to tell them what had happened and to be honest much of it was a blur, so any accurate portrayal of events was never going to be an option. I merely offered them the fact that I needed to clear my head and went for a walk down to the coastline.

One of the guys reached into his jacket pocket and handed me my car keys. I said "thanks" "but where is my car" they looked at each other laughing and said "outside the police station where you left it" I was rumbled. I walked down the station to collect my car. I noticed that the windows were still open, and my wallet was laying on the passenger seat and had been all night. Wow! what a stroke of luck that neither my car nor my wallet had been nicked. I mean who would be stupid enough to steal a car and someone's wallet right outside a police station right?! Well, probably the same somebody who is stupid enough to walk into a police station at one in the morning stoned of his head and ask for medical assistance having driven there in his car whilst under the influence.

I drove to work. As I walked through the kitchen to a rapturous applause and cheering! by all the chefs and pot washers. Completely shocked by my heartfelt welcome back into the world of work the chef who passed me the spliff called me over to have a quiet chat. "where did you go last night?", "Oh I went for a walk down the front to clear my head" he said "no you did not! I know exactly where you were last night" I said, "how the fuck would you know where I was?". He replied in detail my full story of events. He held his index finger up to his closed lips as if to say keep your mouth shut mate. I thought nothing of his remarks of intimidation, but they did play on my mind until breaktime when it all became clear. I was sitting with my housemate during our break, and he proceeded to tell me that the chef and joint rolling nutcase that was threatening me, was Fareham's biggest drug dealer and that his older brother worked in the force and was on duty the night

I walked in stoned off my face. It was all an inside job and probably the very reason they overlooked my arrival in my car under the influence of a highly pure form of imported drug. The penny dropped and everything fell into place.

A few weeks later I packed up and headed home not entirely sure what the next chapter of my life would entail.

CHAPTER 5

AFTER THE STORM.

I was glad to be home despite the obvious lack of family life. It was a strange empty feeling not having my mum around anymore and I know during this time my dad was also feeling the loss, so too was my brother. I soon became, by default, the cook, bottle washer housekeeper and laundry person taking care of the domestic chores in the home. I knew my hospitality training would eventually come in handy. I did not mind at first as it was only right that I should step up now.

My dad had supported me though college and now needed my support in his hour of need. My brother, during this time, was dicking about and had fallen off his own set of rails in his own way and contributed very little to the domestic chores such was way of coping with what happened I guess. It did start to grate after a while, as I was working every day, finishing my placement a year out from college, working at weekends, and trying to maintain some resemblance of a family home.

After a short spell of about four or five months, my mum contacted us to let us know she had moved out of her parents' house and to a small, rented terraced house in the nearby town about twenty minutes from our home. She was anxious to see us, and I guess explain her side of the story, but I refused to go and see or speak to her. I was so angry and upset that she had done this to our family that I could not bring myself to meet with her. Eventually after a few more weeks my brother and I headed over to see her. She was clearly a different person and was equally devastated and upset to see us both. My brother was very relaxed about our time together, but I was furious inside and did not really accept anything she was telling us, although I am sure it was from a genuine place of concern and love for us both. There were tears from all of us and she must have felt a great sense of guilt and remorse as she expressed her side of events.

I left with my brother, feeling no better for the exchange of words, and still felt betrayed and completely abandoned by her. During the remainder of the year, I did not see my mum again and only had a few frequent phone calls here and there perhaps one or two brief visits just to show face I guess but nothing of any meaning to me. Instead, I focused on college, worked at the hotel, and took care of the family home.

As things settled, I became friends with a new girl in the restaurant at the hotel where I was working and finishing my placement. She was a nice distraction from events in my life at the time and I warmed to her quite quickly. She worked for a holiday company across from the hotel by day and worked in the hotel in the evenings and weekends to earn some extra money. I would often be paired with her in the restaurant working our station together and we became great friends. She was a great support to me and a refreshing change to all my past endeavours of finding true love. We would often sit in the restaurant after the evening shift and have a few drinks with the manager and have a bit of a chill out before going home. As she lived in the same direction as me, I would often give her a lift home and that's when things started to pick up the pace. We started dating and soon I had my first official girlfriend. This was the one! I fell deeply in love with her, and we just connected. It was not just the physical connection for me, but for the first time I had experienced an emotional connection of true acceptance with someone also. We were best friends, lovers and did everything together.

She was from a great family. Her mum was awesome and enjoyed having me round as much as I enjoyed visiting. I felt like I had a new family. It felt correct, I felt loved and supported by both her parents who were actively involved in our lives and made the effort to support us both. It really felt amazing to be part of something quite different to what I had experienced previously. We went on holiday together with another friend of mine and his girlfriend to Tenerife for two weeks through her work, our sexual intimate relationship was off the chart and could honestly say I was finally in love. We used to spend hours cuddling together, watching films and just being in each other's company and were inseparable. About 9 months into this relationship, I finished my college course, passing all my exams and graduating. Offers from college friends to take a year out and travel to Australia and India were all for the taking but I declined to live out my days with the new love of my life.

I found a new job as an Evening Service Manager in a local conference and business centre about forty minutes away and settled into my new role and new life, happy as "pig in shit", as the saying goes.

For the next year, things were fine until the love of my life started getting cold feet about us. She became increasingly distant and wanted to spend more time on her own. I tried everything to salvage our connection, but it all came to a head when she closed the door on me one day and refused to talk to me. I was devastated as I had no idea what was going on. Only after two weeks of begging and pleading with her and with the help of her friend that we holidayed with in Tenerife, did she agree to meet with me in a pub in Northampton. I walked in to find her and our friend sitting there, and she proceeded to tell me it was over she did not want to see me anymore. She gave no answers that made any sense to me or justified her change of heart when things had been going so well between us. I just could not understand it. She left the pub angry and upset and as I followed her out to her car she drove off at speed and that was it. I was floored completely. A week later I found out she was seeing someone else.

Her actions sent me straight back to the place I was only a few years earlier, with the same feelings of loss the day my mum left me. Was this some sick joke? why was this happening again? The second woman in my life that I had an emotional connection with had also just walked away from me with no explanation either. Twice in two years I had to suffer the pain of being unloved, unwanted, and abandoned by someone I loved and cared about. I was 22 at the time and this sent me into a deep spell of depression. My best mate was the only one who managed to get me out of this spiralling downward motion, that had it not been for him and his support I would have taken my own life such was the pain I was feeling. We both recall the night he pulled me back from the edge of no return.

What followed was a slow and steady return to a sense of normality with my best mate right beside me. I lost three stone in weight and was on the verge of serious health issues. He got me signed up to the gym, much to my reluctance and he started training with me to build me back up. Within three months I was back to a healthy weight and was exercising three times a day. Swimming in the morning, cycling when I got home from work and in the gym in the evening and this was daily. I was obsessed with my new look, sense of strength and felt like I had risen from the dead. I was in the best shape of my life. I recall walking through the local town centre doing some shopping for some new clothes and a friend I had not seen in a while walked past and couldn't believe what he saw! He freaked out when he saw me. Even 25 years later he remembers that day and we still have a laugh about it today.

On a night out with friends, another mate was telling me that his workplace was looking for new staff and would I like to join the company. I was reluctant at first but having been through the mill and seeking a new change in direction I said yes. I was fed up with hotels, looking after others all the time and was ready to start over. I handed my notice in at the conference centre, where I had been for a few years, ready to start a new chapter in my life. In the same month, another friend's dad offered me and three friends a free two-week holiday in Portugal in exchange for smuggling a large quantity of duty-free cigarettes in the UK. He had a side earner going on with his local boozer, so it was all set and booked. With the events of the previous few years and my life at that point, coupled with my new look and confidence I felt like I was unstoppable and thought fuck it why not! It was me and my best friend, the same guy who pulled me from almost certain disaster only a few months back, his best friend who he played Badminton with and a guy from Leeds University who I had seen a few times when up in Leeds. The four musketeers. It felt that way but probably came across as the lads from the Inbetweeners in reality.

We touched down in Portugal, headed to our modest but free accommodation and hit the town that afternoon and started drinking like our life depended on it. We must have drunk in every bar on the sea front and were all absolutely smashed. I do not recall how or when we got back to the apartment, but we all woke up feeling like we had overstepped the line on the first night. My mate's dad picked us up and took us to a five-star hotel resort where we were able to use the facilities all day. It was not a bad old place to recover form the night before. We sat by the pool all day in full on recovery mode until two of my mates decided they had to sweat it out on the squash court. Me and my best mate decided it was best to sit it out and be as still as we could any sudden movements were not a good idea for either of us.

That evening, shit, showered and shaved, we got togged up and hit the town again, this time a few new bars, a bite to eat and onto a nightclub. Now the club was heaving, full of locals and we were probably the only English guys in there to be honest. The Latino vibe of the music and the flowing alcohol with repeats of club mixes of

51

Ricky Martin numbers "living la vida loca" took its toll on us as we watched the morning dawn arrive from the balcony of the club. We must have left about five in the morning. Getting into the club was free and easy. Upon entry we were all given a plastic card on which to buy drinks. This was new territory for us and the thought of being able to buy drinks without the need to spend our own money should have been a warning sign. One of my friends did tell us to go easy on the cards as you pay for your night when you leave the club. Advice in hand, we ignored our mate's advice and nailed it! What transpired as we went to leave the club was some of us had been rather frivolous with the plastic and racked up quite a large tab to try and woo some local ladies into coming back to ours.

None of us had the money to cover the bill so my mate who initially gave us the warning was the one putting everything on his credit card, so we could leave the club and avoid an almost certain beating by the bouncers in front of us. The walk of shame back to the apartment, which was a good two miles away took for ever, with my best friend so drunk he walked all the way back learning to one side, like a human version of the leaning tower of Pisa. Such was the amusement of his predicament and complete lack of coordination, I don't think I have ever laughed so much in my life such was his struggle that night. How he managed to stay upright was beyond us. His efforts were richly rewarded by suffering backache for a few days after and feeling like he had broken something and wanting to seek full on medical intervention, such was his concern for the daily pain he was having.

Another day at the resort spent trying to ward off the evil that was self-induced comas from the night before, meant none of us were moving from the heat of the sun that day and all of us got sunburn to some degree. That night we decided to have an easy one and went to the English bar just down the bottom of the hill from the apartment. A few light beers and a meal was the order of the evening. The waitress serving us was from Sheffield and as two of my mates were at Leeds University, they promptly began to talk all things northern! She clearly enjoyed the banter and our company that she agreed to meet us the following day for a few drinks. The next day arrived and I was the only one willing to meet the young lady so off I went in search of a holiday romance! The others skipped off to the resort for a day of sport and hitting the squash courts. I walked to the meeting point and met with the young lady and we spent the afternoon together and we really had a great time. We ended up going back to the apartment, got changed and went for a swim in the pool. What transpired as the hours passed was a very charged and enjoyable intimate sexual encounter which resulted in us going back to the apartment for some fun. She made her excuses to leave as she had to work that night, leaving me exhausted and in a state of shock and awe. The lads came back to find me asleep in bed, completely wrecked but amused and somewhat proud of my exploits. We all got changed and headed out again for, yet another drink fuelled night.

The remaining days of the holiday were a constant pattern of repeated behaviour interspersed with the odd trip to my mate's folks house for an evening with his parents and the call to action to discuss the reason why we were all there in the first place. Departure day arrived as I said farewell to my new lover and said we would catch up again when she was back in Sheffield. We were all given an official team England tracksuits and huge kit bags containing the said contraband. As we made our way to the airport for our evening flight back to Blighty. Arriving at Stansted airport late in the morning dressed as team GB there was no probability of being stopped by customs or getting caught with the said contraband and we sailed through without issue or suspicion. It was a well thought out and cunning plan for sure.

Arriving an hour and half later at home, we all said our farewells to each other and went our separate ways as we were dropped off at our respective homes. Following that holiday, I gave up the gym and my training regime I had set myself and decided to focus my efforts on my new job instead. I kept up the cycling for a few months, but the demands of the new job soon left little or no time to commit as I had previously. My new job was working in the Exhibition sector, travelling the UK, building, and erecting exhibition stands for clients and attending set ups for live events. No two days were the same and the work was creative and enjoyable despite working fourteen-hour days most days of the week.

I was earning good money and enjoying my new career path with a great bunch of lads. We were a great team who always delivered and were rewarded well for our efforts by the company. Despite my obvious success with the job, my dad felt it was time I contributed financially to the upkeep of home and paid my way. I had no issue with this and agreed to pay my share. It soon became apparent that my brother who was of an age where work was an option and could have been, chose partying and being on the dole as his option, which obviously meant he was exempt in my dads' eyes for making any contribution at all. It was not long before me and my dad fell out and I went out and bought my own place to live. I left home with a bad taste in my mouth leaving my dad and brother to sort themselves out and I was now with a mortgage, own place, good job and my life ahead of me - I was free at last! I had made it too.

What followed in the following two years was living life to the full, working hard, playing hard, loving hard and trying to find that one person to settle down with. It was time to search for that someone special again. I had a few short-term relationships, all of which were based on sexual exploration rather than deep fondness and love for someone.

I guess living the bachelor lifestyle I was keen to push the envelope a little and explore as much as I could before settling down. During this phase I was curious about all sexuality and was open to pretty much anything. One lady from my new place of work caught my attention and was a complete opposite my usual type. We hit it off immediately and we became very close very quickly. She had a boyfriend at the time who lived in London, which meant taking anything further between us would have been difficult and she admitted that whilst she enjoyed our time together and wanted so desperately to be with me, her feelings for her boyfriend far outweighed the feeling, she felt with me. As she had moved away from her boyfriend for work, she felt our relationship was company for her in a strange place. For me it felt a lot more and I told her as much. We pursued each other, often spending time together at each other's places and taking lunchbreaks at work to be together. There was a sexual tension between us that we explored but never went further than just messing about.

For the first time in all my sexual relationships I was able to fully express my sexuality with her on all levels and she felt the same way. Being able to express our sexuality with each other felt very liberating and freeing and there were never any judgements made or feelings of fear about it. guess for the first time I felt myself in a sexual context with another person who also felt comfortable. I was seriously falling for this woman and tried my very best to win her over but nothing I did was working. One Friday evening we all went out on works night out, a few select friends from work and my new lady had her friend come up and stay with her for the weekend. We proceeded to head to the local bars and nightclubs ending up back at my place. Me, my mate and these two creatures of sensual attraction. My mate kipped in the lounge on the floor of my flat and the two women slept in my bed. I was going to hunker down in the spare room on the floor, but it was suggested by the two women that I should sleep in my own bed with them also.

There I was in bed between two women. One of whom I was in love with deeply and one who was equally appealing. I could not quite believe my luck! All sorts of things were rushing through my mind as these two ladies semi-naked, writhed about either side of me in my bed. Should I reach out and make a move? If so, which one? My lover or her friend? I lay there in a complete state of arousal but frozen solid about what to do, say or think. I am sure that the same thoughts were rushing through their minds or at least I would like to think so. Nothing materialised as we all drifted off to sleep, only waking in the morning to much amusement about the events of that night.

My mate who slept on the floor started to quiz me about what happened as the women left to go home and chill out for the rest of the weekend. He was not happy with my obvious lack of focus on the situation that presented itself in front of me that night. Within a few months I was saying goodbye to the one of the most amazing women in my life to date, who decided to return home. We spent one more night together before she left but I never got the chance to make love to her. I think in our heart of hearts, had we acted out on these desires she would have felt the connection that neither of us were prepared to fully accept and what that might lead to at the time because of circumstances.

I settled back into work having lost yet another woman that had meant the world to me in my life and wondered where now. I knew that I was fed up with the shallow emptiness that were just lust-filled sexual encounters and by now wanted something that was genuine and for the long term. Marriage, kids, house, cars, the whole nine yards and I guess the programme and belief that this is the way to eternal happiness and fulfilment - such is the social programming around this topic in most people's lives. I had played the field and had my time experiencing all I thought I had to experience and now was the time to search again for that one thing missing in my life.

I had seen some friends marry and settle down and knew it was my time to do just that. I really had no idea what I was looking for to be honest, such was my history with the fairer sex. I knew one thing for sure and that I had to be physically attracted to that person, there had to be that spark that instant realization and a feeling. But I also knew I did not just want to settle for anyone just to fill a longing inside of me. The months rolled on and I had sort of accepted that if it were going to happen it would. It is funny how now, on my spiritual path, I can see the universe and divine timing was at play when the woman I met came into my life. It all happened for a reason and why I sit here now some eighteen years later and write this book. All this time, it was God, the universe, my spirit guides, all planning my life out for me and teaching me the values and lessons in life that I would need to grow.

During this time both my parents now completely separated had both found new love too. My father was re-married to a Japanese lady who was highly intelligent but was as mad as a box of frogs and my mum was in a relationship with a man who had recently lost his wife. She had worked with him for some time and now he was retired. Both were happy to have found someone new to connect with. My dad's marriage, I always felt, was one of convenience rather than true love and for the younger Japanese lady, a reason to obtain citizenship of this great country. I said as much to him as I refused to attend his wedding at the time. There was still an air of bad blood between us following me leaving home, and the circumstance which surrounded my departure at that time, and I guess my reluctance to attend this wedding was perhaps my way of payback for the shit he put me through and relying on me to be the replacement for my mum when they separated to maintain the household. I know that not to be the case now but at the time that is how I felt and what I believed to be true. Besides the thought of the new family wedding photos was not one I felt comfortable with. Me and my brother and dad all dressed in kilts and the bride to be in her Japanese traditional wedding attire made for an interesting dynamic for a photo shoot in front of the local registry office on the big day, and not a snapshot in my life I wanted captured on film. I hope even now my dad can see the humour in this situation.

My mum had bought a new house and was a few miles away in the neighbouring town and was now content with her own home and new partner who had also moved to a new house to be nearer to my mum. As a devoted Catholic my mum's new partner was never able to fully commit to my mum and join her in wedlock following the death of his previous wife, so they lived their relationship in separate houses a few hundred meters from each other. I know my mum wanted that new commitment but accepted the fact that it was what it was. I know they were both happy to be in each other's lives and were together for twenty-three years before he sadly lost his fight for life and the angels took him, only a few years ago.

My dad, a few years into his new marriage, was having issues with his new wife and no sooner had their journey started, within three years, he was divorced for a second time and having to fight to save the family home and his livelihood at the mercy of the crazy frog ninja from Japan. Whilst I am sure my dad will share fond memories

59

with this woman and agree it was something, he too, also had to experience. I can't help feeling that cultural differences and shared values were not aligned and the fact my father had not healed fully from my mum probably were very strong factors in the demise of his second marriage. My father a year or so later went on an met his third wife yes third! Now, on all accounts she was a very loving lady, very giving and always happy in the home environment, always cooking, baking, and making the home a great place to be. Finally, my dad had someone to take care of him and his needs again and characteristics like my mum in many ways. They married and seemed to be settled and happy for a good number of years.

CHAPTER 6

A GIFT FROM THE UNIVERSE

It was July 2003 when my life changed in the way I always hoped it would. I was struggling financially, as in 2000, I had left the exhibition industry world and set up to run my own business working as a consultant for my father, overseeing the family business as he was now heavily involved in charitable work and had been for many years, (perhaps his spiritual calling). Times were not great and the money I was getting, was barely covering my bills and my debts accumulated from the previous four years of the bachelor lifestyle. On Saturday the 12th of July one of the guys wanted to celebrate his birthday and he called me to invite me out for a night on the town.

I was skint and really could not afford to go out. He said it didn't matter and that him and the lads would all chip in and buy me drinks. Feeling quite low and really not up for it, I dragged my sorry arse out to celebrate his big day. We were always there for each other in times of need as I guess all friends are. Friends are always there to pick you up when you need them the most. We set off into the local town which was packed solid such was the summer vibe. We spent the night drinking dancing and generally having a great evening. It was about one in the morning and we were standing outside one the pubs deciding where and what to do next. Some of my friends wanted to go on to the club, others more pubs and some wanted to go home. To say an argument ensued was an understatement, everyone voicing their preferred choice and opinion but no one really taking charge of the situation fully. I stepped away to one side and let them sort it out for themselves I wanted no part of the discussion I just wanted to keep moving wherever that was, I had really lost the will to live at that point.

Turning and walking away to find somewhere to sit, I noticed a woman sitting down on the pavement, cigarette in her mouth searching for her lighter. She was rummaging through the pockets of her denim jacket in search of that flame. (my twin flame) I stepped forward and offered her my lighter such was her need. She sparked up her cigarette and handed back my lighter. I lit up too and sat down next to her. Little did I know that this was the one! And I do not think she knew either what was to come.

We started to chat, and I asked her who she was out with. As she pointed to a group of friends who were also in what looked like the same situation as my friends, all trying to decide where to go next. Like me she too just wanted to keep moving. We sat together and puffed away, exchanging polite conversation when I asked her where she was from. She mentioned my home village where I had grown up, I was gobsmacked! "I said no you're not". She said, "how do you know?" I said, "because I have lived there all my life since the age of ten and I know everyone in the village and don't know you". We laughed as she then began to explain she had just moved into the village with her friend who was still meters away ranting about where to go next with her friends. I asked her whereabouts in the village and as she told me. I knew the house she was referring to and her new neighbours. As we sat there conversing it was clear so many things were aligning and so many factors were completely aligned and hard to comprehend. We shared the same birthday month of January - she was born on the 7th, me the 11th. She was Italian and I had been a sales manager for the largest Italian leather tannery in the world at the time. She had been working in a restaurant chain as a waitress in the evenings at a time I applied for a job at the same restaurant as a manager. There were too many similarities and coincidences to ignore between us. Not to mention the synergy of both of our respective groups of friends embroiled in the same set of circumstances. Not only were these discoveries hard not to accept between us. I was completely knocked out just how stunning she was.

She was different in every way. To start with, she was a brunette, Italian and totally knock out. Conversing with her was a major moment for me. Dressed in tight denim bell bottom jeans and a western style blouse with denim jacket with some heels. Half rock chick, half country singer. I was in love instantly. I could not take my eyes off her. A good twenty minutes had elapsed, and both of our group of friends were still in deep heated conversations about where to go. So, I asked "do you fancy coming back to mine?" Without any hesitation she agreed. We said goodbyes to our respective groups of friends and made our exit together as we walked away still in deep conversation. On arriving back to mine we sat down and carried on talking whilst having a few more drinks.

It was probably about three in the morning when I asked if she would like to stay the night. To my surprise she did, and we went to bed and spent our first night together. I will never forget the scent of this woman's perfume, the warmth of her body next to mine and the connection I was feeling. This was completely different to anything I had felt before. We woke in the morning, chatting over a coffee and planning our next date, which was both exciting and very much a time I was looking forward to. I would say we both felt an intense connection with each other. The next few weeks we dated, and things just got more and more intense over the weeks we communicated. Our dates were planned around the fact she advised she had just ended her previous relationship and had a young son who was two years old. Despite this obvious barrier to the relationship in the traditional sense, I was fully committed to this woman. I accepted the situation fully, not really knowing the future implications or challenges ahead such was my love for this woman. I could tell she had a caring disposition and had a huge heart and was going to be a life partner. We dated for about 6 months whilst trying to establish a way forward together in a fully committed experience.

We would often stay at each other's places and spend nights together. On one occasion she came to my place, we went out with my friends and had a night in the town drinking, and I wanted her to meet my mates. They had seen her the night we had met but none of them knew much more than that. To be honest my mates didn't really pay much attention to my newfound love as they thought it was just another notch on the old bed post. But I knew different. I

65

realised if she were to be a part of my life then my mates would need to approve, and she would need to approve of them too. What ensued was her drinking all of us under the table on shots of Tequila. This woman was savage! One of my mates who was the one with the biggest bravado was the first to fall that night much to our amusement. All my friends instantly approved or her! At the bar one friend said, "she is awesome mate, stunning and she has a fantastic arse" do not fuck this up! or me and you are done" Heeded by the warning and in total agreement with my friend's assessment of my new lovers' credentials I took notice of his warning to heart.

As my friends fell by the wayside one by one on this evening of drinking, we made our excuses we headed back to mine. We immediately started to undress each other and went to bed passionately engaging with each other in all manner of ways until what can only be described, as the universe playing more tricks on us and decided to create an earthquake to happen at the exact point of ejaculation whilst embraced with this divine creature. We both felt the earth move quite literally. Now obviously the amount we had drunk that evening and the intensity of our passionate exchanges, it was hard to say for certain if what had just happened and felt was true in the physical sense.

We woke in the morning to local news reports detailing the earthquake that was felt across the county. It was true! We fell apart laughing and bonded even further in that moment. I guess at this point in the relationship I was now with someone who aroused me on all levels, mentally, emotionally, physically, spiritually, and sexually but was also quite a free spirit and quite liberal about life.

66

My relationships to this point from other experiences formed in my mind, a judgement that this woman would meet all my needs and wants in life such was my experience with her to this point. There was no reason to doubt in my mind that this woman ticked every single box for me.

Another first for me was to babysit for the first time, what I now know to be my stepson. This young child aged two, was dropped off at mine as his mum went out with friends. She dropped him off and proceeded to tell me his routine and left for a night out. I guess for her it was a true test of my ability to be who she wanted me to be. Could I cope with a two-year-old?

I will not lie and say I was completely out of my depth at this point, but me and the little fella had a riot. His usual routine went straight out the window and I did whatever I could to entertain this new addition to my world. It was a baptism of fire for sure and a moment I will cherish forever. I felt some comfort that despite having only dated for six months, my other half was already at ease with leaving her son with me on my own, which must have taken some blind faith and acceptance on her part and gave me a sense that this was true commitment on her part and that all my feelings and emotions about this woman were true and valid and from a place of genuine trust.

She returned later that evening with her son safely asleep and asking a hundred and one questions about how we got on. It was a great memory I still hold dear to this day. A few more months of dating and spending time with them both only solidified our connection. It was decided that I would sell my place and move in with her, back to the village where I grew up. The irony of this was that I spent years trying to escape the quiet village for more excitement and experiences, only to return to a place I knew was comfortable and familiar. I sold my home and with £32,000 in the bank I was set for this journey. Now despite my obvious windfall from the sale of my own home I was some £28,000 pounds in debt. Not an ideal situation for sure and my choices at the time regarding my finances were questionable to say the least. I paid off one of my loans and bought a new car with the remaining funds. My family advised me not to sell my place and to hang on to it, advice I wish I had listened to. But such was my commitment to my new relationship, I was prepared to sacrifice everything for this new woman in my world and the love and happiness she was bringing to my life at the time. There was no doubt or question in my mind that this was everything I had been looking for and some.

I moved into the cottage in the village with her and we began our journey together. Making friends again with our next-door neighbours who I had know most of my life in any case. Everything just felt comfortable, and everything just seem to fall into place.

For the first few years everything was as it should have been. We were both deeply in love with each other and loved the situation we were both in. To celebrate our first year's anniversary date, she booked a night out in London to see MOBY at the London Astoria. Now for me this was all new territory. I was your typical country lad, never fond of the big smoke and the hustle and bustle of big crowds despite working in the city in the exhibition trades such was my experience to date. It was my first gig in the big smoke and although excited and keen to expand my experiences with this woman in my life, it still felt a little out of my comfort zone. It was a great night with great music, and we left the club around midnight to return to the hotel. It was one of many experiences we would share over the next seventeen years together and each one I can say brought its own unique experiences. Some good and some bad. It was shortly after this celebration I plucked up the courage one evening to ask her to marry me. It was in our cosy cottage, the open fire was on, we had just had dinner and my stepson was fast asleep and we were snuggled up on the sofa deep in conversation. Now it probably was not the most romantic of places but sometimes you just have to make that call, my intuition was telling me not to wait any further. I did get down on one knee as I asked the question and to my surprise she said "yes"!.

The first test of our relationship came when I decided to return to the Exhibition trade and return to my old place of work. My own business was not delivering the results I was seeking, and the lack of steady reliable income was causing issues. Taking on a new senior position in the company, I was welcomed back with open arms by my previous employer. It felt good to be in a place with some stability as I built this new life and family around me. After a year or so I became despondent with the job and the company and things were getting to me. The management of the company had changed in the four years I had been away from the business and I started to lose my passion for the work and the business. The role I was in, meant I was faced with many challenges of trying to do my job, not helped by a boss who was a complete tyrant - unsupportive and was only interested in the bottom line rather than the welfare of staff and in the end the stress was too much for me and I lost my shit and I walked out one day. I was told I was suspended following further investigation.

What transpired was three months of seeking another job and taking the employer to Industrial tribunal, which I later found out they had been subjected to several times by other employees. I should have won my tribunal case based on legal technicality, but it went in favour of my employer. So, I was left wondering just how much the director of the company was paying the judge. My satisfaction came from seeing all three directors and the HR manager facing questions from a disgruntled employee under oath. For me it wasn't about the winning, although the settlement figure would have come in handy at the time. It was more about seeking a fair outcome to an awful situation that was forced upon me.

Obviously, this situation placed a great deal of stress on our relationship as my partner took care of all the bills etc. as I struggled to find new work. I knew I would find work but the three months I was out of work was a stressful time and the cracks I guess, started to show. Looking back on the situation now I can see and accept the concerns my partner had. The lack of my support - both financially and emotionally during this time were not present and resentment and her frustrations were for sure justified. I guess we were worlds apart on this situation. Her view was one of I had a family to support, and my actions were selfish and incomprehensible in her eyes. My view was that I was not happy and that a change was needed. I could not be who she wanted me to be in that situation, however selfish my decision was at the time.

I can see both sides of the story but me being the arrogant male in the family and standing my ground I pushed through regardless. Family life and security had been threatened and I guess this was irresponsible in her eyes. I guess I was hoping for her to be more supportive, but the way I was raised and my stance on things, having witnessed my dad take risks in his career, I felt sure of my intentions.

I managed to secure a job with a local events company on the sales side of things in March 2006 and we were back to normal. The lack of progress in the relationship took its toll on both of us and we often fought, about money raising my stepson, who was now testing both of us and the right way to raise him having both come from different upbringings and wanting our choices to be accepted as the correct way. We would often make it up to each other and decided despite the problems we were facing we would again celebrate out anniversary on 2nd July 2006. Another concert was booked, and this time it was a stadium gig to see the Red-Hot Chilli Peppers at Ricoh Stadium, Coventry. It was an amazing day and fantastic gig, followed by a night back at home making out and repairing the damage we had both put each other through over the recent months.

We attended the Greenbelt Festival held at Cheltenham Racecourse with my Dads charity to support and offer some assistance as volunteers in August of that year. We checked in to a local B&B in Cheltenham. It was during this trip that we walked past a jewellery store and I bought our engagement rings on the spot. A chance purchase to seal our relationship and my commitment to my partner, such was the want to make her my wife. I recall her reluctance to join me in the shop and the shaking and her feeling unwell as she was being measured for the ring. We went out for dinner that evening to Raymond Blanc's restaurant and had a great evening whilst managing to escape the restaurant, not having to pay for the wine, as they missed it off the bill and sneaking out the fire exit like a couple of delinquent teenagers, such was the challenge to avoid the costly bottle of plonk! Returning to the hotel we again spent an intimate night together to seal our commitment and promise to each other earlier that day.

For the remainder of our stay my partner felt quite ill and decided to stay at the hotel as I continued to support my Dad at the festival. Now I don't know if her illness was from the food we ate, or her reaction to the realisation that she had now fully committed to me as my wife to be. Looking back, I think the latter was probably more the reason for her downturn in condition. The rings purchased had seven small holes filled with rubber and I promised that for each year we were together I would put a rock in one until it was full. The idea behind that was that if we made it to seven years and still wanted to be together it was destined to be. I was all too eager to avoid the "seven-year itch" that most couples face and so this was my way to acknowledge that destructive belief in some way. Sadly, I never did live up to my promise to put a rock in each space on the ring although we reached and surpassed the seven years and went on for another ten but never got married. I guess our souls knew that it just was not meant to be.

Another argument ensued a few months later, when my mother-in-law came to stay and flew over from Tenerife where she was living with her youngest daughter and help raising her granddaughter. Now I guess my partner felt to a degree somewhat abandoned by her mum for moving to Tenerife and raising her younger sisters' daughter instead of staying in the UK and helping her out with my stepson. I had known for some time that my partner's relationship with her mother was a very tenuous one and she often shared stories of her teenage years and the constant battles with her mum who had also been through a series of relationships during her upbringing.

Her time with us, although only a few weeks, soon sparked several arguments and ill feelings, and I was soon being accused of being abusive towards my stepson. Nothing was further from the truth and I ended up moving out and moving back to my dad's house that was only a few yards up the road, until her mum had left and went back to Tenerife. My mother-in-law never accepted me, and the feeling was mutual I guess on some level. I may have triggered her subconscious patterns and experiences she had witnessed during her life and I guess her projections on to me were her own core wounds that were never dealt with or addressed, such was the reluctance to accept me. Likewise, my mum also had issues accepting my partner and felt something was off too.

My stepmother's accusations of abuse towards my stepson in her eyes were only realised by me quite a few years ahead when the penny dropped for me. She had spent much of her working life in the social care system, protecting others from such situations, but what transpired one evening really gave me cause for concern when she was speaking on the phone to my partner confessing that one of her partner's was accused of sexually abusing my partner's sister. My partner was horrified at this and cut all ties with her mother for about a year. Now to this day I will never know the truth of the conversation that took place but was my stepmother trying to say my partner had also been a victim of such events too but was using my partner's sister as a scapegoat to gauge my partners reaction to this confession of abuse. I must say that it would certainly help explain why my struggles to be sexually intimate with my partner throughout our relationship were always such a battle. It also explains that my stepmother was also perhaps party to or witnessed some form of sexual trauma in her childhood and I guess the call to work in social services and her obvious desire to raise her granddaughter having failed in raising her own daughters in a safe environment. It all sort of makes sense to me. Whether this is true or not the realisations from my spiritual awaken and the way I see people and how they present in life in front of me, gives me some confidence that I am right on some level.

Things between me and my partner were at an all time low for a few months, and I spent a good number of weeks periodically staying between my dad's house and at home with my partner to try and get some space to consider my options and contemplate where it was all going wrong. My partner came to see me at my dad's one afternoon and as we sat and talked about how things were going, she broke the news to me that she was pregnant. Holy fuck! I was floored for the second time. I burst into tears and she reached out and hugged me. At this point my head was so far up my arse I really did not know what was happening. Words cannot express just how elated I was but at the same time riddled with guilt for the way the relationship had been with her over the last few years.

I was on top of the world but feeling so bad at the same time, a state of mind I still cannot get my head around even to this day. I moved back in and we both made a concerted effort to unite and put our differences aside based on the circumstances. Now for her to tell me she was pregnant must have been a very hard decision as I had known previously that she had had a miscarriage many years ago with someone and the fact we were not even living together and struggling, it would have been easy for her to have had a termination and walked away from the relationship. I think both of us knew that despite our difficulties and struggles to that point we had something very special between us. We both knew and accepted just how much our own family meant to us, both having come from broken homes. This was our chance to make that dream happen and one we had both dreamt about of all our lives.

We decided to locate to another cottage in the village, such was the need with the pending addition to the family. A place was located and moving date set. All the time my partner showing signs of our imminent new arrival. It was the end 2007 the beginning of 2008, when the world had the big financial crash. Economic ruin for banks financial institutions across the globe were rife and so too was the marketing budgets for most of the companies I was trying to sell events to. A few months after Christmas, end of February after we had moved into the new place I was let go and made redundant.

With my partner 2 months from giving birth and me out of work, I cannot stress how this affected our relationship, but I guess I don't need to spell it out. We ploughed on regardless and I secured a sales job at a local car dealership as an interim solution to my predicament then inevitable happened.

My partner had just bought a new outfit for her work's Christmas party that was delayed because of the financial crash breaking across the globe over the festive season. Trying it on with her new bump on show. Putting her heels on, she looked a million dollars! Glowing in fact. As I expressed my approval with the caveat that was it wise to wear heels in her condition.

The look of disgust and cowl on her face as she slipped on the second shoe and then a change of look, to one of sheer panic on her face as her waters broke!

Now, I had no idea what this meant nor were we prepared for this - it just happened. We didn't attend anti natal classes or read up on maternal procedures. I just accepted the fact my partner had it all under control having had a child already. Perhaps if I had shown more of an interest in the imminent arrival of my own, then things would have been less stressful. But to be fair us blokes are just not built that way. At this point we still had no idea if we were expecting and boy or a girl. We had never enquired during the scans. The shoes were ruined and so too was the new dress. What ensued over the next 6 hours is still a blur. She started to panic and said she needed to get to the hospital. My stepson was crying such was his concern for his mum and I called my dad and his wife to meet us at the hospital.

Jumping into the new company car I had just acquired, we headed to the local hospital. We went straight to the maternity ward. My partner was taken straight through to the ward and was rigged up to some monitors to ensure she and the baby were all well. I stayed for about 30 minutes and then left her to go home with my stepson, who I had left in the waiting room with my dad and his wife. I collected my stepson and we headed back home to pack some things for his mum as we did not know how long she would be in hospital. I called his dad and said I would need to drop his son off at his, as his mum was having the baby. I dropped my stepson off at his dads and made my way back to the hospital.

It was about 11.30 in the evening and when I returned to the ward bag in hand, the bed was empty. Panic stricken with fear I searched to locate my partner. I was led to the delivery suite and on entering the room I could see my partner and my dad's wife supporting her through her contractions and very final moments of labour. Every man wants to be there to delivery his baby and as I held my partner's hand and cuddled her, she put her arm around my neck and held on for dear life. I do not know if this was intentional or just for support, but I was stuck in a headlock for the remaining 20 minutes and was unable to move. I never did get to see the joy of natural childbirth or delivery my daughter into the world. Something I will always regret.

My daughter came into the world after a few hours labour, at 12.05 am 30th March 2007. Natural birth, no drugs and fit and healthy, if a little jaundiced and underweight at 5 lbs - the exact same weight that I was when I was born. I cannot tell you just how amazing my partner was during this time of giving birth. This woman was just incredible in every sense of the word.

My daughter was checked over by the midwife and the nursing staff wrapped in a blanket and handed to my partner. Words will never describe the emotions I was feeling seeing my partner with my daughter, both well and happy. I stepped out of the room to call my dad, my stepson and friends and family to advise them all of the safe arrival of my daughter into the world. With the news delivered to friends and family, I stayed for a few more hours before leaving to go home and get some rest, and to leave my partner and my daughter to also get some. Arriving home at three in the morning I could not sleep such was my excitement. I think I manged a few hours' sleep before waking up around eight in the morning, getting ready to go and pick up my stepson from his dad's so he too could see his sister for the first time.

Everyone was at the hospital that morning to welcome my daughter into the world. At that moment I had my own family with the woman I was in love with and with family around me. My partner stayed in hospital for a few days with my daughter just to ensure all was ok, as there were a few concerns but nothing that wasn't handled without the proper care and attention as you would expect. Fitting the car seat for the first time, preparing milk and feeds at all hours of the day and night, changing nappies all very much a reality now and no longer a dream of mine. This shit was real. For the first few days, with my partner and my daughter at home, my arse didn't touch the sofa once, such was my dedication to taking care of both of the best I knew how.

It was not until day three when I was making my daughters milk in the kitchen that I broke down in tears. The realisation just hit me out the blue and I was an emotional wreck for the rest of the evening. My partner comforted me and assured me everything would be OK. I was starting to question my ability as a husband, father to my daughter and man in general at this point such were the circumstances that surrounded our relationship at that time.

The constant money worries, job insecurity and the fact I had a daughter now and all the responsibilities that that brought with it. The feelings became all-encompassing and pushed me into a place of fear, worry, anxiety and depression. This was only heightened by the fact for three years my daughter never slept through the night. Both my partner and I were crabby and tired, unsure of our direction or if we could find a way past these battles and struggles. Because of my minimal earnings in my current job, my partner decided to return to work as soon as possible. Part of this decision was financed based, and in some part, I guess she wanted to return to work. Subconsciously perhaps she felt could not rely on me to support us in a way she would have wanted me to, which I feel to this day was the real reason. She had four previous failed long-term relationships before me, and I guess each one of those failed to meet her expectations or needs in some way. I cannot help but think had she opened up to me more about her concerns and feelings, then I would have been more understanding and receptive to pushing through my own fears and finding a way to improve things. But I guess we were both in a state of confusion and currently worried about the future. Her past relationships, I guess, each and every time had conditioned her subconscious mind not to trust, not to accept, and not to love someone who wasn't showing up correctly in her eyes.

Chapter 7

MY BREAKING POINT

With my daughter now three, and my stepson nearing the end of infant school, my partner decided it would best if we moved nearer to our local town of Kettering. Her best friends' sister had recently separated from her husband and their house was up for rent. As things were between us, a house move was not on my radar nor financially a good move for me. We were barely making the bills at this point as it was, and with my daughter in full time nursery, it was a stretch to say the least. I was uneasy at first and my partner said it would make her happy to move and perhaps create a new fresh start. I agreed and supported her decision, despite my concerns she said we would make it work. The move took place and we settled in relatively quickly, making new friends in the close where the house was located. In an attempt to earn more money to try and improve our situation, I left my job in search of another. I was out of work for a few months as I searched in vain to locate another job. Which I did eventually but not before the shit hit the fan again.

The stress of kids, the relationship, lack of communication, no job, no money and no real direction about where this relationship was going, I had no choice but bail out following two days of bitter arguing and being made to feel guilty that all this was my fault. I admit that I was lost, had no fight left in me and feeling generally like there was no point to the battles anymore. I went to stay with my mum at this point for a change of scenery as she had known for some time that I was unhappy and struggling in the relationship, and I guess felt obligated to help me knowing what she had gone through with my dad years earlier when they separated. I managed to find a new flat and now on income support with no job, I was single, alone, afraid and feeling like I wanted to end it all. I had failed at the one thing that I wanted most in my life. I could not support my partner, my kids nor myself with any level of satisfaction and my self-worth was at an all-time low. The next few months I spent almost every day in bed, in between searching for jobs and trying to claw myself out of the depths of hell. I did not speak to my partner for about a month and when she said I needed to spend time with my daughter. I said I was not strong enough to do that, but she insisted and dropped her off regardless, forcing me to step up for my daughter's sake. After a few months I wasn't able to pay my bills as my income support had stopped because I had missed a job centre appointment. What I was getting really didn't cover my rent, let alone normal bills for water, electricity, food etc. I was ready to end it all there and then.

To top it all off, I woke late one morning to get in my car to go and see my mum and seek some advice and noticed it was clamped and with a DVLA enforcement notice slapped on three windows of the car telling everyone it was an untaxed vehicle. One of my new neighbours had the decency to report my car as untaxed. I was living in a terraced street where parking was difficult at the best of times and as my car was stationary for most of the time, I guess my neighbour decided to take it upon himself to release one more parking space by having my car towed. I went back inside and broke down in tears for what must have been most of that day. I now felt there was no coming back from this and started to think of ways to end my life, such was the hole I was in. My car was towed away to be crushed, despite my calls to try and get my car back. I called my partner to tell her about the car and that I could not pick my daughter up that weekend and that I was not in the right place to see my daughter. My partner called me back the following day and said did I want to go out with some friends for a few drinks. I said no but she insisted that it would perhaps help me get out of this rut I was in and that we could spend a night together to try and work things out. I was shocked at her suggestion as only two months ago she was ready to bury me under the patio.

Why the change of heart? why the offer from her? It just did not make sense. I decided to accept, knowing that it would be a discussion that I was not looking forward to and unsure if I could keep going through these battles with her. She managed to get family to take care of our daughter and we agreed for her to come to mine. She turned up at 6.30pm, late as always, she was never on time for anything and it used to really piss me off, so already, I was in a bad mood before she arrived. No call or message to say she was running late which left me feeling whether she would show up at all. For about three years our intimate relationship was virtually non-existent, despite my protests to spend more time together and try and be closer to her. I guess what with my daughter now in the picture and a major part of our lives together, with the daily grind and working all hours, she just wasn't feeling it anymore. Despite this I stressed to her on more than one occasion just how important this was to me. I was accepting of our circumstances and situation and just wanted her to make an effort now and again. I always insisted that this was an important part of any relationship. I made a few attempts to rekindle this part of our relationship by arranging nights in and out etc, but it was hard work and never reciprocated on any level. Intimacy with her was my way of feeling close, accepted, loved, and valued by her and I know that the way things were between us and the years of struggles were not conducive to this part of our lives, but I guess I wanted to feel closer to her even more during this time.

29th May 2010 I will never forget how she looked when she turned up at my front door. Long gone were the denim jeans, denim jacket and western style blouse that first rocked my world. There she stood in front of me in a tight, grey fitting, short, ruffled mini dress, black high heels, hair all done made up nails painted and smelling and looking like she had just stepped off a fashion shoot. I was blown away and highly aroused at the same time. Was this the same woman that only a few months ago was full of rage and hatred towards me pushing me out the back door and throwing black bin bags of clothes at me? I felt like I was in a dream. Now I will never know just how stunning she would have looked on our wedding day as we never made that day a reality but let's just say, if I could have had any wish on how she looked on the big day, how she was looking that night would have been my wish for the big day. I have never to this day managed to scrub the image of her and that night out of my mind. It is permanently etched into my subconscious mind. She reached towards me to kiss me passionately as I handed her a glass of wine. The touch of her lips on mine, her perfume and scent of her warm sun-tanned Mediterranean skin were simply too much for me to comprehend. We spent the next couple of hours making out in various rooms in my flat. I simply could not get enough of this woman in my life. Suitably re-charged we got ready and went out with our friends for some drinks. We both got amazingly drunk, and our friends were always trying to get me shit faced, and that night they achieved it with gusto. Walking back to my place in the early hours of the morning, we were discussing joint wedding options with our friends, such was the feelings of togetherness from all of us. Me and my partner got back safely and spent most of the night making out again until we both crashed and burned, falling asleep next to each other once again.

We both woke in the morning feeling a little worse for wear and spent some time discussing our way forward again. I went outside the back door and stood in the morning sun having a cigarette contemplating what the last twelve hours had all meant to me and just how could I live up to my partner's expectations. As I leaned against the window, she came out to join me drinking coffee and taking in the sun. I was looking at my life in front of me as I dropped my cigarette and my head in shame and burst into tears sobbing uncontrollably in front of her. She asked me why I was crying and held me tighter than she had ever done, comforting me and telling me she loved me and that everything was going to be alright. It's no joke that in that moment she had just saved my life and I make no

86

joke about that prospect. I was in the darkest point of my life so far, and the one thing I wanted the most in my life had just pulled me back from the edge.

It's almost as if this woman was my guardian angel, sent to test me and protect me in equal measures. I knew she was a strong woman, but this was off the chart and perhaps why I loved her as much as I did and why the intensity of our battles hurt so much. We spent a few hours that morning making out again before she left to go home. I do not think in all the years we had been together I had ever felt so vulnerable and connected to her at the same time. The next few weeks were spent arranging a time for me move back home to be with my family where I should have been. Moving back home was a strange feeling but one I was glad to be doing. I was more than determined than ever to sort my shit out and pull myself back together and be the man she wanted me to be.

Life carried on and things started to settle down and things became stable for the first time in years. There were still battles over money life kids etc. some worse than others but we had a newfound understanding and acceptance of each other. There were times when we had the odd argument, and I would inevitably walk out of the house and spend the night in my car, such was my refusal to battle it out. Yes, it was selfish of me and stubborn and perhaps an immature way of dealing with the issues, but I was fed up with fighting with the woman I loved. I decided that we perhaps needed some help and to that extent we found a local relationship councillor and we went a few times. Now I was determined to be open to this, to try and find the answers or reasons for our constant battles.

It lasted a few sessions before I stopped it because she was not showing too much interest in the homework the counsellor had set us to do. To me, it felt like her lack of intention was something she felt she didn't need or want, and I think on some level it would have exposed things that perhaps she wasn't prepared to open up about and hence her self-sabotaging this step forward for us both. We stopped attending the counselling and we carried on regardless but at that moment I knew on some level, her commitment to our relationship was being questioned. I too, had a sense of doubt about how we could get things back on track.

Life from this moment on became stagnant for both of us and we were trapped in the daily grind of raising two kids, working all hours to make ends meet and paying off debts and never really finding any relief from the reality we found ourselves in. We were drifting apart each day. I wanted us to get back to that place where we were when we first met and wanted more intimacy and connection. As for me, that was my happy place. I felt loved, valued, appreciated, and connected to the woman I was in love with. I guess she wanted excitement, stability, new adventures, and a way forward to grow together but sadly, neither of us were able to find it within ourselves to relinquish that control over each other's feelings and our own wants and needs during this time which only led to more and more frustration and resentment towards each other. Each of us blaming the other for the way things were going down. The only thing that remained consistent was our anniversary 12th July. Every year we made a conscious effort to buy tickets to see our favourite band together the Foo Fighters! A soundtrack to our relationship for many

88

years and the one time we came together, regardless of the events playing out before us in our lives. It was always a time we both looked forward to and one memory I will always treasure.

My stepson was now a fully fledged teenager and was like most, completely addicted to computer gaming and online time. This was starting to adversely affect his schooling and drove a wedge between me and my partner, to the extent that he was out of control and refused to go to school each day having spent most of his days from 3.30 pm till the early hours of the morning, stuck to his screen and never really engaging with the world. I can see how our relationship was affecting him and I guess this was his way of dealing with what was happening. Both me and my partner agreed this was not good for him and fought like a pair of kids over the best way to resolve the situation and restore some balance to his life. Forced intervention with his dad and the school caused again some ultimatums for me and my partner to the extent that I said either his computers goes, or I go, such was the stress of the situation for us all. Lucky for me his computer went on this occasion, but I can still recall the hatred my stepson had towards me during this time, and the lack of acceptance by my partner that I had forced her to make this decision against her own son.

As we all know, teenagers who do not get their own way will often step up the fight and cause more issues. My stepson was no different. Despite my best efforts to communicate to him some valuable lessons, he was hell bent on pushing my buttons most days and trying to get me to react. He would often lash out at me or attempt to fight with me in the physical sense and my daughter was

89

pretty much witnessing all of this and experiencing these turbulent times. Trying to balance my daughter's welfare and that of my stepson's aggression was a difficult time and anyone who is in stepfather-stepmother relationship will know just how difficult it is to not overstep that boundary during times of conflict, especially when there is more than one father or mother figure in the relationship to deal with. My stepson's dad was worse than useless in trying to assist in his son's welfare at this time, refusing to accept any responsibility for the events that were playing out before us all, despite the fact he was the one who lavished his son with the gaming computer in the first place. His dad just used to throw money at him I guess to smooth over the cracks of the fact he was not part of his life for much of it. I guess because I was fortunate as a child growing up and had all I needed as a child, I felt on some level I would not do that for my kids. My time, I felt, was always more important rather than materials things. Unfortunately, because of my relationship battles, much of my time was trying to be close to my partner than it was spending it with the kids.

I decided to take a back seat during these times of conflict and allow my partner and her ex to sort this out as my efforts and opinions were clearly causing more harm than good. What developed was a natural family separation within the home. My partner taking care of the welfare of her son and me taking the welfare of my daughter and never were all these dynamics cohesive on any level. A "them versus us" mentality was developing. Me and my partner were so distant from each other during this time that any normal loving sense of a relationship was so far out of reach, things naturally started to drift even further apart.

We hardly spent any quality time together and what time we did spend together was with her friend groups or trying to keep the family dynamics together despite the troubles. We were no longer intimate together and this was devastating for me such was my desire need and want to connect with her on this level. Most nights consisted of me watching the TV, both kids upstairs doing their own thing and my partner in the kitchen or on her the phone to friends or family and doing anything to avoid any interaction with me. I would retire to bed most nights about ten pm leaving my partner downstairs drinking and falling asleep on the sofa only to coming to bed in the early hours of the morning. This was not the life or relationship I wanted for us and despite several attempts to ask her to come to bed early and or make the effort with me, it was done with much reluctance and through gritted teeth in some attempt to keep the peace. I was longing for that intimate connection with her again and expressed this on many levels and occasions but to no avail.

It was my 40th Birthday and my partner booked a nice hotel in London and we planned a nice get away in February 2014. I was amazed at the effort she had gone to and I was again amazed just how much she could turn the situation on its head. From one moment feeling distant and cold towards me and then pulling out all the stops to show me how much she did care. This was very much the dynamic of our relationship for years. Periods of fighting interspersed with moments of sheer joy and happiness and willing to come together. We arrived at the hotel and spent the afternoon walking around the city taking in the sights and taking in a bite to eat. My partner had surely done her homework to make sure this was a weekend and night to remember. We returned to the hotel in the late evening and sat in the bar having some drinks. We knocked a fair few back as we conversed for the first time in months. I wanted to go up to the room for some intimate time with her, as it was only occasions such as these that we found this time together, but she was more than happy to stay in the bar and get pissed up. I stayed for a few more drinks and then we agreed to retire to the room. What followed was more disagreements and finally an all-out war and being accused of having an affair. Now I don't know why or what she felt she was trying to do to me, but my reaction was one of disbelief and shock. I asked her to justify the accusations she was making, and she told me exactly how she was feeling and what she felt I had been up to.

What transpired was her feelings about the way she felt at the time I moved out of the home and was living on benefits. During this time, I had reached out to an old school friend on Facebook as she too had just separated from her husband. We were old school friends and the fact I had not seen or even spoken to this woman since I was 13 at school was my partner's own insecurities about our relationship. I never met my old school friend, I never wanted to and there was no attraction on my part at all. It was just a shared experience and conversations about relationships or lack of, that we were both experiencing at that time. I assured my partner that nothing was going on nor had there been, and that if she were that

92

sure of her accusations, I would kindly give her my friends details so she could call her and ask her for herself. I had absolutely nothing to hide nor would I. I left the hotel room and went for a long walk to calm down. I must have been gone a few hours returning to the hotel bar at three in the morning and continued drowning my sorrows in a few more drinks.

My partner text me to ask where I was, and she came down to the bar to talk to me. We had a few exchanges of words and retired to the hotel room to get some rest. My partner apologised to me and wanted to be intimate with me, but I was too far wasted and tired, not to mention upset, to even contemplate any interaction with her on what should have been an awesome time together. We must have woken about nine in the morning and went down for breakfast. I was still in a state of anger and resentment towards my partner about her outburst, and full of emotions that again, on another significant occasion, I was facing another set of traumatic turn of events.

We went back to the room and made out for what was the best part of the day to re-address the imbalance of the actions the night before. We headed out late in the afternoon for another stroll around the city, taking in the Tate Modern and other cultural attractions. We returned to the hotel and spent most of the evening together intimately reconnecting and trying to overcome the scars of what had happened. On returning home things were restored to normality and life carried on as normal.

There was, by choice, an obvious distance between us now following that weekend and over the course of the next few years situations were popping up that really questioned both our resolve in the relationship we had with each other. I had never felt so isolated, alone or unloved in all this time with her and the pain I was feeling was causing me depression, anxiety and a lack of direction on how to fix the situation between us. It seemed that whatever I did nothing was having an effect. Physical intimacy between us happened rarely, and when it did it was always acted out under the influence of alcohol on her part. Now I understand a good drink gets rid of some of the inhibitions in people, but this was a pattern of behaviour from her I was not willing to accept in my life anymore. I was making love to someone who had numbed all the feelings and sensations most would like to feel during these times and for me it just felt false each time. I soon turned to interacting with women online, such was my desperation to feel loved and accepted by someone. I did not want to be intimate with someone who had to be shitfaced to engage with me. To some degree I felt a great sense of injustice in her accusations of an affair and felt perhaps exploring other options might be something to consider such was the direction of our relationship at this time. I soon connected with a woman from my old college days who was also going through a similar situation with her partner and what started as a light relief soon became a highly sexual charged connection between the two of us. Although I never engaged with her during my time at college there was a connection of sorts between us. I knew what I was doing was wrong but at the same time if felt so right. I guess my situation was no different to anyone else going through the feelings of lack of self-worth, self-hatred and filling that void. Most will turn to an addiction of some sort. For some it is alcohol, for some it is drugs, for some it is sex, and for some it is eating anything that gives us a short-lived comfort to restore the negative emotions we feel from time to time.

I was no different to most, as my relationship was on the verge of the precipice of freefall. This was my coping mechanism and always had been. What transpired was a few months of interacting with this woman and filling that void as my relationship was on the rocks.

In my misguided and flawed judgement, I passed my address to this woman and she decided to send me a racy letter in the post together with a gift, and it arrived and was opened by my partner on a day she chose to take off work. Now I had no Idea of the pending doom I was about to face but I received a call whilst at work from my partner, clearly very upset and angry, saying that she needed to see me urgently. I left work and travelled home to what can only be described as the wrath of Satan incarnated. I was immediately set upon by my partner asking me to explain what had been going on. I knew that I had to be honest and confessed fully what I was doing, there was no way to hide my interactions with this woman online nor the evidence that was being presented in front of me. I knew at this moment my relationship was over and that what I had been accused of only months earlier on my trip to London was now very real and my reality for my partner to deal with and accept in me.

I was riddled with shame, guilt, frustration, anger, resentment, and any other emotion and feeling you care to mention. I offered my apologies and justifications for my behaviour and I explained that such was the relationship with her at the time, I felt alone, unloved, and not worthy and that what I was doing was my own selfish way of dealing with these emotions and feelings I was having. I wanted nothing more than the rekindled passion and feelings with her that I had once experienced and that trying to restore that with her was pushing me further and further into my lack of self-worth. I assured my partner that this would stop and that my attention and focus would be totally on us going forward. My partner forgave my actions such was her belief in me and my desire to make things work between us, and that in all honesty was all I had ever wanted for us both. I was in love with her no one else and by this time my life with her over some 14 years was all I ever wanted. My issue was trying to love her in the way I always had.

Now, despite my actions which I deeply regret, she too had given reasons to question her trust on a few occasions. Like the times she went out with friends and never came home at night which happened on a few occasions, or whilst I was packing away and loading a van with equipment on the final night of the one of the four Isle of Wight festivals we attended I saw her kissing some random guy pissed out of her face, not to mention the deep-seated subconscious reason she told her ex why she ended the relationship with him was that she had had an affair. A concern and worry in me I carried all this time in my mind that this could happen to me also. A thought never far from recall, in times when our relationship was in trouble. I guess to this day and I know for sure that she too was not fully honest with me about times she had wondered or strayed, and perhaps her reasons for her forgiveness at this time.

I can say without doubt and I swear on my daughter's life that in the all the years we were together I never once touched, kissed or physically met another woman whilst with her. There were times for sure when the grass always looked greener and more tempting, but I never took that leap of faith to find out. I set my intention for this woman the night we met. That this was the woman I wanted to spend the rest of my life with and that was a commitment I was willing to make. I wonder if she could say the same. I still to this day believe we were completed devoted to each other, despite our slip ups and in the seventeen years we stayed together. I know I would have been able to forgive her for any events that caused pain and hurt, such was my attachment to this woman who was a huge part of my life and made me who I am today. We put the past behind us, and both agreed to make a concerted effort to try and restore what we once had. As the years passed, more events tested us but at the same time brought us together equally. It was without doubt a rollercoaster of emotions. Extreme highs and the lowest of the lows. We seemed to be trapped in this cycle of events and patterns that neither of us knew how to deal with or correct for the betterment of our union. Both of us trying to control each other and the outcome we both wanted but never fully being able to surrender to each other. One of us always had to be in control of the situation and hence the deadlock and fight.

I just wanted to love this woman and for her to love me it's really that simple, and all I ever wanted. Little did I know all this time we were both self-sabotaging the relationship because of our programming and beliefs in our own subconscious minds.

CHAPTER 8

HER BREAKING POINT

We tried in vain to hold our family together whilst on this rollercoaster, but the bloody thing never seemed to stop, and neither of us could get off. I recall one evening her coming home from work and as she walked in the door, I could see she was distressed. She dropped her handbag on the side and went and sat in the garden without saying a word. I went out a few moments later to see if she was ok and could see that she was struggling to breath. She was clearly in a real bad way and in a blind panic. I had never seen her struggling with anything before, well certainly not to this extent. I called an ambulance such was my concern for her and her obvious condition.

The ambulance arrived and the crew set to work on her connecting her to all manner of machines and equipment as me and my daughter looked on concerned and worried for her. My daughter started to cry. I gave my daughter hollow assurances that everything was fine, and that her mum would be OK but, on the inside, I was just as scared as she was. There was some relief to my partner as one of the paramedics was an old friend of hers and with this in mind, she was somewhat comforted by the fact that this guy was making her feel less anxious during their checks. Some light-hearted banter about friends made for a less stressful time for all of us and put her mind at rest to some degree.

She was taken to the local A&E department for further help as the paramedics were not convinced that she would be stable if left to her own devices. I arranged to drop my daughter off at my Mums and went straight to the hospital to see her. Arriving at the hospital she was on the trolley in the corridor, waiting for a bed in the resus ward which was not a good sign. I stepped outside to make some calls and advise friends and family what was happening although at this point, I had no idea of the severity of what was happening and the very thought I might lose her was a very real and conscious thought racing through my mind. She was taken into the resus department and given a bed where she stayed for two days. I never left her side.

That evening I sat beside her all night and into the early hours of the morning contemplating life and what this all meant now. What if this? what if that? All manner of thoughts racing through my mind. Here was the strongest woman I had ever met reduced to nothing, but a sleeping shell of a person, hooked up to all manner of machines and drugs. It was my biggest fears that I might be losing the woman who was always there for me and had given me everything. Despite regular checks by the staff and cups of tea and coffee to keep me awake throughout the night, I sat by her side - nothing could take away the fear that this might be it. She woke in the morning, still in much pain and discomfort but talking and told me to go home to get some rest. I said no but would leave for a few hours to go and see my daughter and friends to assure them that she was still OK but not well. I returned to the hospital a few hours later and again stayed by her side, never wanting to leave in case she lost the battle. At least I would have some comfort in my mind that I was by her side as she had been by mine should the angels decided to take her from us.

The kids were brought up to see her and spent some time with her reassured that she was awake, talking, and conscious. After a few days she was transferred to a ward where more family and friends came to see her. I think on the fourth day I was confident that she was going to be OK and went home to get some rest.

I carried on dealing with regular life back home and making daily visits in the evenings to spend time with her. After a week she was discharged and sent home to recuperate for as long as it took. To this day, I still do not know what her diagnosis was. She never said, but I can say with all certainty she was not the same woman anymore. Her recovery was long and arduous and with daily medications to take for weeks after. A situation I know she hated as this woman never took any medication for anything. She was clearly frustrated at her condition and inability to live the life she had always done and that frustration at times was clearly taken out on me on occasion. I accepted that fact and could see that she was not blaming me, just merely frustrated at the situation. Maybe she was blaming me on some level, but she never said as much. This moment I think was the turning point for her in terms of our relationship. Added to this situation the onslaught of menopause and her complete lack of need for any intimate relationships, fast approaching fifty and a general feeling of not having achieved where she felt she wanted to be in life, I guess it all took its toll. She had been giving to others all this time and felt in someway it was now time for her to receive the good stuff.

Despite an almost full recovery and further medical check-ups and tests that year, life carried on as normal. She was still drinking, and despite being advised to stop smoking which she did for about 3 months on medical grounds, things soon got back to normal, and she carried on living life to the full, grabbing every opportunity to do things with friends and family. Despite her new lust for life, she still refused to spend quality time with me as I had always wanted her to. The remaining undertone of togetherness that I had always strived for with her still not being taken as valid or even considered from my point of view. It was clear to me that she was not going to do anything she felt she did not have to do anymore. The overriding feelings I felt was that this was her time now and fuck everyone else approach. She didn't say as much but I knew deep down that was her thought process and feelings at the time. No sooner had she recovered from her stay in hospital, the pain of our relationship was clearly still influencing her ability to consider our relationship with any sense of normality or wanting togetherness.

We were now so distant with each other there was very little or no communication from an emotional level. Anything we discussed was about the events of the day and the weather, any excuse to avoid any deep and meaningful conversation about us and the relationship. Now despite having found a stable job, money was ok, and a sense of stability had surrounded us for the first time in years things were only getting worse between us. She took a few days off work as she was feeling a little unwell and returning home one night, I found her on the sofa in the lounge crying. I was obviously concerned and thought the worst. Had her condition flared up again, had she had some awful news what an earth was going on. I had no Idea, and I knew it had nothing to do with me this time. She proceeded to tell me, after much persuasion, that earlier that day she had had severe toothache and as such decided to relieve the pain by pulling three of her own teeth out. I had known for years that she had an irrational fear of the dentist and never went in all the years I had known her - only once when she needed urgent treatment, but this was on another level. I was completely shocked and disturbed at the fact that she was now completely out of control of things and struggling to deal with life.

I cannot tell you how upset and angry I was feeling that she felt she had to go to these lengths to deal with what she was going through. She had been there for me when I needed someone but here was someone clearly struggling with life, love and the whole universe and trying to cope alone. I still do not understand why she felt she could not rely on me anymore. Perhaps my lack of support in her eyes in the beginning of our relationship formed a belief in her that I was not able to step up. Or maybe her programme of having to be sheer bloody minded and miss independent all the time was more the issue. The following day I took her to see the dentist for a check up and see the effects of what she had done. I knew that if she didn't go and get this checked and she had an infection of some degree she would be in a seriously bad way. She took it upon herself to make a further appointment to have the work done. I took a day off work and we went to the dentist for what I can only describe for her as another trauma event. Whilst under a general anaesthetic for two hours she had all her teeth removed in one go and dentures fitted.

Leaving the dentists with false teeth and bleeding gums and in pain, I could not even comprehend she took another month off work to recover. The cost of the treatment was paid for by my stepson's dad who offered to help financially, and he felt obligated to on some level as my partner had only a year earlier taken out car finance for my stepson to get him a car as his dad couldn't get any finance. So, it was his way of paying back that generosity, I guess. A further period of recovery for her and her struggling to deal with things were starting to take its toll on our relationship.

She was fast approaching her 50th Birthday and a major milestone in her life. I guess this was her facing a midlife crisis and seeking to make a better life for herself. I know deep down that somewhere I wasn't going to be a part of this and think by this point she too had the feelings that she needed a new direction and a way out of what was clearly not serving her anymore. With the looming birthday celebrations, I chatted to her best friend to discuss what we should do. We all knew that she had been struggling for some time and that I felt in some way to blame for some her struggles. I wanted to make things right for once and set out to make it a celebration like no other.

I said to her friends I wanted to do something special and a bit different. My plan was to have a mini festival with big bell tents, mobile bar with a DJ and a field with tents for guests to stay in. I had made some enquiries with friends I could call on to help make this a reality and everyone was happy to chip in. Her friends on the other hand had already booked the venue and paid the deposit for the venue, bar, and DJ, without telling me. I was angry to say the least that they had not taken on board what I had wanted and decided to do what they had preferred instead. This obviously caused a major blow-up ahead of the celebrations and yet again I was the arsehole for not going with what her friends had planned. I gave up and let her friends take over what would have been my way of giving back to her for all the shit times we had been through. Neither her friends nor my partner had any validation or agreement for my wishes. At this point I knew I was simply fighting a dead end. I couldn't get through to my partner on any level, she wasn't interested, and I was alone in all this.

I decided to take a rain check and instead plan twelve months of things to do each month for the year ahead. Now the fact we hadn't had a date night or any significant time alone together in the last few years except for our annual pilgrimage to see the Foo Fighters for our anniversary, I felt doing this would show her I was committed to making the effort to restore the balance in this relationship. January was obviously her birthday month and mine too, but this was her big year, so I gave away any thought of my celebrations to ensure we celebrated her Birthday, and I was OK with that as I knew my 50th would come in good time.

I arranged weekend getaways, meals out, gig tickets to see the Foo Fighters in Glasgow as part of our annual trip to visit my dad in Scotland where he was now living and had been for some years. She also had a trip to New York planned with her best friend so by all accounts it was going to be a great year, or so I thought.

Her birthday party in January organised by her friends went without a hitch but had been tainted by my falling out with her best friend over the event for which she never forgave me for. Our trip away that was supposed to be a romantic getaway, was more like a reluctant trip with a resentful teenager who didn't want to go away with its parents and was spent mostly drinking in the local pub and not really conversing more over watching the Welsh kick England's ass in the six nations on the big screen surrounded by cheering Welsh fans. And me falling asleep alone in bed whilst my partner sat up most of the night refusing to get close to me on any level.

The local gig got cancelled due to the band cancelling and the meal out at the local restaurant never happened as the voucher we had been given to use was lost or misplaced. Her trip to New York went ahead as planned, so too did a girl's trip to Croatia to celebrate one of her friends' birthdays, also too the holiday and annual family trip to see my dad with the Foo Fighters concert thrown in for good measure. The rest of the events that year simply did not materialise at all.

In September, our relationship had completely stalled, we were not talking, she was distant and cold, and I was spending more and more time on my own. Things had taken a turn for the worse on all levels. I knew something was wrong, but I just did not want to have another battle with her to try and bring up the conversation we so desperately needed to have. In my heart of hearts, I knew this was the end of what had been my life for seventeen years.   She continued to sleep on the sofa and found every excuse to go out at weekends with friends as she put it. In October she attended a school reunion party, and this night re-ignited a relationship with someone she had previously had feelings or even a relationship with before. That night she came home, and I noticed her getting out of a white BMW with two blokes in the front. It was the early hours of the morning and I was still up, concerned as to where she was. She had told me many times she would be back by a certain time but in recent years that had never actually happened. On occasion it would four in the morning, and I would be trying to call her to see if she was OK. I was generally concerned for her as my partner, a mother of my daughter and of course for her own wellbeing, knowing the shit she had gone through with her health in recent years. I knew on some level that she felt my attention towards her during these times was smothering and controlling but nothing was further from the truth. I just wanted to know she was safe and OK.

When she came into the house, I greeted her and asked her why she was so late and who were the guys dropping her of she said sorry for being late and said it was a taxi. Now I knew full well it wasn't a taxi, coupled by the fact she was so pissed she could barely stand up I knew and so did she that what she was saying was complete bollocks. I asked her to come to bed with me and she refused point blank. Deciding to sleep downstairs that night, whilst I lay upstairs wide awake knowing that this was the end.

In the morning she made her excuses and spent the whole day out with friends again. She never told me where she was going or what time she would be back. Despite trying to engage in conversation with her about what was going on and could we sit down and discuss things, as evidently, they had got to the point of no return. I was met with refusal and rejection at every turn. Every weekend from that night onwards she would take off for the weekend, leaving me at home with my daughter, who was also asking questions for which I had no answers of any truth or validity to calm the fears for my daughter's concerns. The next two months were sheer hell! Knowing my partner was sleeping with someone else and lying not only to me but her daughter too, was just not fair on any of us. She moved into the spare room to avoid any physical contact with me and refused to talk about anything when questioned. She knew what she was doing, and she knew it would cause nothing but grief, heartache, and pain for everyone involved. In her mind she was done!

Early December and with Christmas fast approaching she relented and came out with the fact she no longer wanted to be with me. What ensued was two hours of her shouting and screaming at me about my infidelity, cheating on her and the fact she wanted more out of life and that there was no way to resolve our relationship. It was projection after projection from her about my shortcomings, which were in fact a reflection of her own mind and actions. A point she still fails to accept. She told me she wanted me to move out and I said that she would have to wait until I had found somewhere for both me and my daughter. A bedsit or staying with my mum was not an option for me. Least of all I had a legal right to stay in my home until I had found suitable accommodation.

I decided it would be best for me to travel to see my father in Scotland during the Christmas holidays. As much as I wanted to be around my family at this time of year and resolve our differences, I knew this was not going to happen. I booked my tickets and headed off to Scotland telling my daughter what I was doing, as my partner had no interest in anything I had to say at this point. My life had fallen apart in the most cruel and selfish way and it was a point in my life I was never wanting to face. Whilst the years with her had been a rollercoaster of highs and lows, this woman meant the world to me and I guess always will, on some level. he gave me my daughter which I guess is the thing I am most grateful for.

I knew my time in Scotland was needed. It would be a time to adjust facing my life on my own and having to deal with what laid ahead of me now. I had always held on to the belief that whatever me and my partner had been through we would always find a way back. We had proved that time and time over the years and I honestly felt this was no different in some respects. I was leaving for Scotland hoping that upon my return and with some distance between us things might just be able to move forward. But I also knew that there was every possibility that this was also the final chapter to my journey with her.

CHAPTER 9.

SOLITUDE AND REFLECTION

I arrived in Scotland having travelled by car, train, and boat to the Isle of Arran where my dad lived alone following a messy divorce from his third wife. That's a whole other story. He was waiting by the drop-off point as the ferry docked into Broddick. The whole journey that day was one mixed with a sense of sadness and reflection. It was the same journey I had taken many times with my partner and daughter when our family visited to see my dad. It was always in August and we always celebrated Christmas Day as it was never realistic to get all of us together at Christmas time, and the weather was always an issue up in that part of the world with the ferry crossing in the wintertime. It was part of our annual event which sadly would be no more.

A happy family affair in the usual sense of what was now, very much part of my history. It also brought up feelings for me about my last trip with my partner to celebrate our seventeenth anniversary as we did every year watching the Foo Fighters at Bellahouston Park in Glasgow and the last time we shared an intimate connection. Seeing my dad as I left the terminal building had me bursting into tears at the mere sight of this great man in front of me, who he himself had not only faced every kind of adversity but had been in my position three times now and was very open to my obvious distress.

We set off on the 30-minute drive round the Island back to his home. Me telling him what had happened and what was going on. We settled in the lounge after some dinner, and I began to open up to him in full what was really happening.

He was the first person I had emotionally opened up to about my troubles, and he sat, listened and offered his words of support and wisdom. I messaged my daughter to tell her I had arrived and asked her if everything was OK. I couldn't talk to her as I was too upset, so messages were exchanged as a way to hide my pain and make everything feel OK for her. I am sure on some level she needed me to be by her side during this time and for the love of Christ I wanted to, having been through my own issues of abandonment and just how it affected me, but I was also conscious of my decision to leave was probably not the best for her.

I knew that I needed me to be OK with things before I could be sure I could support her. I was justified in leaving, knowing that had I stayed at home something would have kicked off further and that it would have caused more pain and suffering for everyone which was something I wanted no further part in. Every day I had thoughts of loss, grief and just how fucked up this whole situation was. I tried day after day to come to terms with what had happened to my family and face every dark thought and memories of joy at the same time. I knew my time in Scotland was my only way to accept and deal with the fact that this isolation I was feeling in that moment, would more than likely be my reality when I returned home. After a few days I settled in and felt more at ease with the circumstances I was having to face. Long conversations with my dad about the past and his relationship with my mum and how things went south with them too, was some comfort and acceptance that things are never what they seem. I guess for me it was the first time I could see my mind had made thoughts, feelings and judgements about actual events that were false in every aspect. Some of my dad's words made many emotions and feelings about my own parents' separation that I had been holding on to all this time fall away with some relief and gratitude on discovering the actual events, that I guess were never really discussed at the time. I had a new sense of clarity and understanding about some feelings and emotions that should have never been there in the first place.

I made a call to my daughter on a few occasions checking in with her to see if she was ok and to give her some reassurance that I too, was OK. My first real moment of sadness came on Christmas Day when my dad was dishing up Christmas dinner. I was standing on the porchway to his house having a cigarette, feeling empty, hollow, and completely alone in the world looking out over the water when I broke down in tears. This was not how it was supposed to be. My dad came out, put his arms around me and said everything would be OK. I knew it would be in time but in that moment, it felt like I had just been pulled right back to the starting line again and had to start the race all over again.

We ate Christmas Dinner and despite the sombre atmosphere we shared a moment in time that was now part of my story. I called my daughter to wish her Happy Christmas and check she had

113

received the few presents I had managed to sort before leaving. Boxing Day was just another average day for me in this distant land and taking my dad's dog for a walk, as I again contemplated life and what the future would hold for me. Being in Nature, at this time, was very humbling and so far, removed from my home. I was grateful for the nature that surrounded me, and I was feeling peace in the moment however isolated I was feeling.

Most evenings were spent in the lounge with my dad watching movies or listening to music and talking and reminiscing on times gone by. I would turn in for the night most evenings about ten o'clock as was my usual routine but fully clothed with a hat on such was the state of the weather at this time of year and the lack of heating in my dad's 100-year-old Victorian abode.

The next day I borrowed my dad's car and decided to head into the local town for some cigarettes and a few bits of shopping. On my way back from the town I stopped off at a local beauty spot. This was a pilgrimage for me of sorts and one of a spiritual connection to my partner. Every year we went to the same spot and took a selfie of the two of us. It was one of those things we just did and something to reflect on as we grew old together. It was lashing down with rain, freezing cold and blowing a gale as I walked over to the exact spot and stood reflecting on the memories of that moment. Now I don't mind saying that all my life I have felt certain connections or synergies with events that are presented in front of me, and this very moment was no different. As I stood there in the pouring rain, reminiscing on the moment I shared with my partner in the exact location, two white swans came swimming round the corner.

Now for some reading this I am sure you are thinking so what? but for me it was a sign. The last time I had been in this spot the same thing happened, two swans were swimming in the sea just yards from me and my partner. I sat and pondered on this event and concluded that it was a sign that me and my partner were still connected in some way, despite the obvious car crash of our relationship that had resulted in recent months. With some comfort in that event, I got back in the car and drove back to my dad's house. The next few days I reached out to my partner to try and speak with her. It was a very calm conversation for the first time in months but still she refused to open up fully about what was going on. Sticking to her story that she wanted to be alone and that she no longer wanted to be in a relationship, and that she wanted new things in life. Despite the obvious lies and front she was putting on I knew this was complete bullshit on her part. She did offer a little more wisdom to me upon questioning, and I guess she felt safe to do so, knowing I was some four hundred miles away.

It was New Year's Eve and by this point I was feeling ok. It was decided that me and my dad would go and celebrate in the pub a few doors down from his house. With about ten locals in the pub, it was a low key but enjoyable evening with much of my time conversing with the landlord and my dad, interrupted by a few lads out fishing that night who decided to jump ship and come into the pub for few bevvies. There was a woman who had travelled halfway across the world to visit the pub that night as she used to work in

115

the pub years ago and it was a real sense of longing that inspired this woman's journey. It also gave me a ray of light that I was now free to do exactly what I wanted should I choose to do that. I was not tied to family commitments or a relationship anymore. A few moments before midnight I stepped away to call my Daughter to wish her a happy new year. We spoke on the phone as she broke down in tears. I apologised to her as my heart sank hearing her sob at the end of the phone. I asked her where she was, and she said her mum's best friend's house as was often the case. (The friend I had a fallen out with 12 months earlier over my partners birthday party) I asked where mum was, and she said at another party. Her mum's friend came on the phone and assured me everything was fine. It clearly wasn't and I was livid that my partner had fucked off to spend time with this new so-called friend of hers leaving my daughter alone and without anyone to be with her. I know I had taken the time to get away, but had I known my partner was going to leave my daughter with no one to be there for her own selfish reasons I would have stayed with my daughter. I didn't think my partner could be that selfish. But then she had been that way for the best part of two years now, so it was hardly a surprise to me. But hey what did I know?!

I tried to reassure my daughter that everything was going to be fine whatever happens, holding back my own tears. I returned to the pub and began to wish complete stranger's a happy new year. Despite a sad point in time, I felt truly part of a group of genuine, humble, and caring souls all wishing me the best for the new year. It was a small but important comfort to me. I felt more connected to

116

these complete strangers than I had been with my partner over the last few years.

We carried on drinking for another hour or so before heading home and calling it a night, going to bed and ready to face the new year. Waking up feeling a new start and a new year, I knew deep down this was going to be the toughest year of my life to date. I wasn't due to go home until the end of the week, but the weather was closing in and I needed to bring forward my journey home due to the ferry's that might be cancelled due to the incoming weather. As much as I enjoyed my time in Scotland, it was the right call for me based on what was happening in my life. The isolation was welcomed as it gave me a sense of what would lay ahead, it prepared me for being alone. I popped into the town again for some more supplies before my pending departure and again decided to swing by my spot in nature to reflect on my thoughts once again from the last few weeks.

The weather was overcast and windy but no rain. I walked down to our spot and looked out across the water again only to be greeted by a single swan now swimming in front of me. This again, was to me my confirmation that I was to face the next year alone and that I was no longer part of something I was holding onto for dear life at this point. I caught the first ferry off the island and glad I did as it was the only ferry off the island that sailed for four days, so I would have been stuck had I not made the call to set off early. On reaching Glasgow central train station, I was in for a two hour wait before my train journey home. I didn't want to hang around so purchased another set of tickets to commence my journey earlier. I wanted to avoid arriving back home late in the evening straight into arguments having spent all day travelling. A few train changes and I was nearly home pulling into Northampton train station.

I text my daughter to tell her I would be home shortly. She replied telling me she was not at home and would see me later that evening. I was so looking forward to holding her in my arms and being with her again. I recall the drive home, trying to be calm and rational about whatever unfolds in front of me to remain mindful and calm and not to let whatever happens get to me. I remember pulling into the driveway and walking to the back door to let myself into my own home. Now it was always a concern that my partner had changed the locks, she had done it previously when we had experienced bad times, so I was relieved to find my key still worked. Unloading the car and walking into my home was a strange but awkward feeling and several emotions came flooding back. As I sat down, I waited for my daughter to return.

She walked through the door about nine o'clock that evening and she ran straight into my arms as I had expected she might. I asked her if she was ok, the smile on her face gave me my answer and all the justification I needed. There was no welcome home from my partner not that I was expecting one to be honest. My daughter went upstairs and spent the evening in her room, I guess glad that I was back home. I can say despite the frosty and cold reception, I was also glad to be back with my daughter. I made no attempt to reach out to my partner, remaining seated in the lounge waiting for some communication. She came in and sat down and started to make small conversation asking me how my dad was and what had

I decided about how to move forward. I asked her if the time apart had changed anything in her mind, and I could see that nothing had. I asked her to again tell me what was going on and why she no longer wanted this. The same reasons were given that she wanted to be on her own and needed different things now in her life, that our relationship was no longer worth saving as too much damage had been caused. Despite my objections to what she was telling me I asked her to reconsider. I decided to turn in for the night and found all my clothes had been moved into the spare room now. I accepted this move and kept myself to myself for the next few days not really engaging with her on any level. We managed to converse one night, and she wanted me to leave the home immediately. I said that I couldn't do that and wasn't prepared to be thrown out of my own home, not at least for my daughters' sake. I expressed I wanted to do the separation fairly and with the minimum amount of drama for all concerned. She set an ultimatum and a date she wanted me out by. I agreed to pay my share of the rent weekly until I was to move out. Such was the date on my removal from my home I was tempted to fight for my right to stay in my home but knew it would prolong the suffering and none of us wanted that. It was my partner's birthday again and despite the hatred she was showing towards me I bought her some roses and a card as I did every year. I placed them near the kettle in the kitchen so when she woke up, she would see them first thing. There was no thank you or acknowledgement on her part initially only a small "thank you for the flowers" as I left for work walking past her to go to work. I don't know what I was hoping for as a result of my gesture, but I guess me showing I still had

119

feelings for her, despite the shit she was putting me through, might have resonated with her on some level, but it clearly had no effect.

This was one cold hearted bitch who was only interested in herself now. Despite my best efforts my partner daily tore me a new arsehole, making my presence in the house so unbearable to such a point, I guess she was hoping I would just pack up and leave like I had done previously. But this situation was very different and we both knew that. My focus at that time, was trying to resolve our differences with one goal in my mind and that was to avoid putting my daughter through a separation. I knew just how much this situation was going to affect my daughter and how much it had affected our lives from our own experiences of family separation. I spent the next few days viewing properties with a view to buying or renting, although I knew buying was just out of reach for me at that time. I was hoping that family, my dad, my mum and brother who had fallen on good times would be able to support me at this time to enable me to make a new start. I located a new flat and borrowed some money off my brother and his wife, and my dad to get my deposit paid, pending approval and reference checks for my new flat. It was a rental option, as despite my best efforts, my family felt rental for the short term would be my best option based on the circumstances and financial position. It was more expensive than I had been paying where I was and added to that the bills, I would now have to pay I wasn't sure if I could manage the extra outlay. It was a stressful time for sure, but I knew it was only a matter of days before my ultimatum would kick in and had no choice to push through my fears and just do it.

I advised my partner I had located a place and that I would not be able to move for another couple of weeks. Despite this communication she kicked off and decided that evening I was to leave that night. What ensued was again two hours of her screaming and shouting, pushing me around and threatening me with eviction with help from my stepson and his dad. I decided such was her rage and obviously mental state, I would gather some clothes and leave that night. I went upstairs to my daughter, who was in floods of tears to tell her that her mum wanted me to leave tonight. I held my daughter in my arms and held her tight and tried to reassure her that everything would be fine. It was not the first time she had seen me leave home in this way, so I guess she was somewhat used to the events that were taking place. I hated every minute of it and had done each time we fought. Most of the time it was alcohol fuelled as my partner hit the vino to try and numb the pain she was feeling. This was her addiction to cope with her emotions again. I recall one night she was so drunk and violent towards me, I had to call the police to enable my safe passage to leave my own home. During that next hour, I got as much stuff together as I needed to take and began loading my car. I said a final goodbye to my daughter knowing that it would be the last time she would see me at home. I called my mum and asked if it would be ok to stay with her. My mum had, over the years, always been there for me and had often been a safe place for me to go when faced with adversity in my relationship at times. My mum was clearly expecting my call at some point and welcomed me into her home without question. Just like my mum, I walked out on my family, not through choice but because of circumstances.

121

I broke down in tears, and just like my dad, my mum comforted me in my hour of need. It was real. It had happened, and I was now without a home, my family, and my life as I knew it to be. I had many conversations with my mum over the course of the next two weeks about what had happened and my feelings towards her and how I felt when her and my dad separated. This was a difficult and emotional conversation and one that should have taken place twenty-four years ago. As a result, I realised I was supressing feelings and emotions all this time. I did say I also felt that it is history repeating itself and that it felt like Groundhog Day.

What I witnessed when I was twenty-one was my own story repeating the same pattern some twenty-four years later, the similarities were uncanny. My mum offered me a home for as long as I needed, to enable me to save some money and pay off some bills, but she was also recently suffering the death of her long-term partner and I knew despite coming together with her after much time and having open conversations, it really wasn't the best place for me to be whilst dealing with my own grief and life events. We were both suffering a loss of immense magnitude. My mum felt my immediate departure was not the right choice and wanted me to say longer but I offered my honest reasons and explanations for my departure as soon as possible inciting the fact it wasn't her it was me, and my own healing I needed to come to terms with. I moved into my new flat February 7th, 2020 at 12-00 midday. With money left over from my dad I bought some second-hand appliances and some basic furniture. I picked up my daughter and showed her my new home for the first time. She had her own room and bathroom, and finding the right place was key, as it had to accommodate her needs more than my own. Sadly, my partner was not able to see the importance of this and the reasons for the slight delays at the time. I got my daughter a key cut and said she welcome to stay any time she wanted as this was her home too. I made no issues about where she should stay and hoped that she would want to spend time with me as things got easier with time.

I settled in gradually and was at peace with my surroundings. It was quiet well located should my daughter want to come after school and close to town where she would hang out with friends at the weekends. It was perfect. The irony of the location was the fact it was less than two hundred meters from my own flat I had sold years earlier to be with my partner. I had come full circle right back to the start again. I felt a sense of calm, knowing I was alone and could deal with the fall out in my own way and on my own terms. I made a few attempts to call my partner and arrange for further items to be collected from my home. A few days were all I needed to collect the years' worth of belongings. To say I had my stuff all over the house was an understatement and I knew I would have to leave some items behind as I was not given access that I needed to ensure a full search was made to make sure that I had everything, and to be honest, the less I had the better.

A few months in and I was almost settled and beginning to deal with the emotions of everything that was happening. I was told by my partner not to contact her and to stay away from the house and not to turn up to see my daughter. Any communication between us would only be because of my daughter's welfare. I tried a few times to reach out to see if I could get some honest closure about our separation, but she refused to engage each time as I suggested it would be for better for all concerned. She said if I did not leave her alone, she would get family involved or someone to prevent me from contacting her or even get a restraining order on me. Now I know why she was behaving in this way, she had shown this behaviour pattern to her own mother in the past and her sisters, when they had upset her and pissed her off. It really didn't come as any surprise that she would behave in the same way with me, it is her default setting. Sometimes people find it far easier to walk away from the pain and suffering than actually face it. But a restraining order was the icing on the cake and confirmed to me just how insecure she was and showing herself to be, not to mention she was having an affair and I guess wanted to make sure she was not caught out by me turning up unannounced to see my daughter. It was all a big smoke screen to avoid the truth on what was going on.

She had known for some time that she wanted out of the relationship and had prepared for every eventuality in her own mind and based on past experiences of failed relationships, so I guess she was only doing what came natural to her. It did upset me, that she felt this harsh towards me knowing we had spent seventeen years together, had kids and family etc. All I wanted was some honest communication and some closure, but she never wavered in this, despite my occasional conversations to ask her to be open about what was going on. I knew deep down that she was seeing someone else - all the signs were there. I think to this day that she still had feelings for me and did not want to hurt me anymore, so her refusal was her way of protecting me from the truth on some level. It was also her way of dealing with the separation not to talk about it. She did say that in one conversation had she spoken to me about it she might have changed her mind and she knew that she could not stay on the rollercoaster with me anymore.

I do not know why I was so insistent on seeking the truth from her. I knew we had not communicated our feelings to each other for years so why now? What good would it serve us? I guess for me I just wanted to understand why. Anything to take the pain away of losing the woman I loved and always had. I did ask her one question in a final attempt to seek that closure and her answer I guess would seal the deal for me. "do you love me?". She refused to answer. I knew she did and always had done, and to this day still does but I guess with us both living with the programmes and patterns that were in both our subconscious minds the universe stepped in and decided we could not be together until we had learned the lessons of the past. I guess on some level I also wanted the woman in my life who was prepared to walk out of it, step up and speak her truth and be emotional available for the first time. This was the third time in a row that I was abandoned without a truthful explanation.

CHAPTER 10

COVID-19 & SPIRITUAL AWAKENING

As I can continued to work and deal with the fall out, my boss and work colleagues were advised of my situation, I felt only right to inform them of my demise at this time. My emotions and feelings would almost certainly bubble up and slap me in the face at work whilst trying to carry on normal life. On a few occasions at work, I struggled, having to remove myself from the office to catch my breath and deal with the enormity of the emotions I was feeling at this time. As much as I tried to suppress my emotions during work, it sometimes was simply too much to bear. I cannot express just how supportive my colleagues were during these initial months, some of whom were faced with even harder life challenges than me.

We were heading into March 2020 when it was announced the country was to be in lockdown due to COVID-19 pandemic. I was immediately furloughed from work and the only thing that was keeping me going at this time, was work. I was now forced to sit at home alone, isolated and with no distractions to pass my time. My partner refused me any access to my daughter, such was the threat of this pandemic which I felt was completely unfounded but again just went with it to avoid any further issues with her. I was not in the mood for more fights. I just wanted, during this time, to be with the one person who was my world and that was my daughter, who I had not seen since I showed her my new home that day. I was also concerned for her welfare knowing just how mum was coping during this breakup. I knew she would be drinking and doing everything possible to avoid dealing with her feelings and emotions. I felt that it was only fair and just, that my daughter should see me during this time. Seeing her during this lockdown would have perhaps enabled me to focus on the one thing that was still important to me. Despite my requests I was pretty much told to "fuck off".

I sat for the first three weeks in March in a state of despair, regret and again, questioning my life's purpose. Some days were worse than others and it got to a point, I was daily contemplating my own existence in this world. Now I had been down this path before of questioning my own life, once with the first love of my life but I had my friend save my arse. And once with the woman I loved beyond all comprehension who was now no longer part of my life. My friend was going through his own battles and my partner was no more. The two people who knew me the most to help me deal with this were not around to help. I was on this path alone this time. My Mum, brother and my dad all offered their time for me to vent and speak up if needed. I was grateful for the support at this time. I did often pop and see my brother and his wife and quite often expressed how I was feeling, sometimes breaking down in tears in front of them, also too with my mum. My best mate was always on hand anytime I needed him, but as he was facing his own divorce battles and had been for five years, I guess my troubles would have only added to his pain too, so I thought carefully about reaching out to him. I had been there for him over the last five years and knew his story and it was far worse than mine, but we always had each other's back. He was a support to me at this time and I suppose knowing his journey and shitstorm he had faced and still was, I had learned some valuable lessons on not what to do to deal with my shit.

I had booked a session with his counsellor to vent my emotions and feelings to someone who would not make any judgements about me and whilst I broke down in tears as I expressed everything, I knew it was not helping me get the cause of this pain. The pain and suffering was identical to what I had felt on previous occasions, when I had hit hard times whilst in relationships, only this time in my head it felt a thousand times more real and threatening, as I guess I had the responsibility of my daughter to consider. I really did not want to keep feeling this pain or deal with repeating cycles in my life and I wanted answers. I really wanted to be the dad she needed and deserved, and I wanted her to be proud of me. I was not sleeping, eating, or looking after myself for many weeks and I was on the verge of seeing my doctor to get some prescription medication to perhaps ease the pain. As I dialled the number to book the appointment, I knew it was not the right call to make. My soul knew had I taken that step, it would have led me down a completely different path and so I hung up the phone and sat staring out of the windows, searching for some inspiration or an idea to help drag my sorry arse back to normal in some small way. I went to bed that night about ten that evening. I was so tired and exhausted that I drifted off to sleep almost immediately. It was the first time since being kicked out of my home that I managed to fall straight to sleep.

Now anyone who knows me will tell you that when my head hits the pillow it is "light's out". Not much would normally wake me up, so what happened next really shook me to my core. I woke up at exactly three in the morning. I recall looking at the time on my phone, I was wide awake and felt like I had been awake all day. I felt as fresh as a daisy, no ill feeling or grogginess having been asleep for some time, it was as if I was alive again. For a few moments I could not quite understand why I was feeling this way or why I was so awake. I got up and went into the kitchen, returning to my bed a few moments later to try and go back to sleep but I was **REALLY AWAKE**!

I spent the rest of the morning not sure what or why this was happening and despite my frustrations of being awake at this unearthly hour, I spent the rest of these hours until daybreak on my phone scrolling and scrolling watching youtube videos and passing the time. At eight thirty that morning, as the day was waking up, my phone bleeped. I made my way to the Facebook notification tab where a message had been posted for my attention. I clicked on the link and was taken to a post about Experiential Healing and the founder of this work was a guy called Duke Sayer. I was completely baffled by this arrival. I clicked on the post and watched this guy's video in its entirety. He proceeded to explain about his own life journey about dealing with chronic back pain and how he overcame years of suffering, despite medical intervention treatments of all kinds, and nothing had helped. I was fascinated by what he was saying and very sceptical about the post, not to mention the validity of this content. Was this another spam post or scammer. He was offering a free five-day challenge to change your life and initially I thought what a crock of shit and carried on scrolling. I sat and pondered my own position in life and felt a call to sign up, much out of curiosity than anything else. I guess the fact that I was seeking some way out of my own suffering and I had just awoken from a deep slumber to a state of consciousness I had never experienced, before coupled with the strange appearance of this Facebook post, I felt I had no choice but to engage. I signed up and as I was off work on furlough, I could throw myself into this challenge and see if what he was saying would have any impact on me and my own life. What transpired in the following five days is the very reason for me writing this book and was the beginning of my spiritual awakening.

I was accepted into the group and joined Duke on a live pre-challenge group feed on the Sunday evening, the day before the challenge commenced. To my surprise there were hundreds of equally intrigued participants spanning the globe from Canada to the States, Australia and from continents far and wide. We all listened to his words of wisdom and I quickly became very attuned to what he was saying, although not fully immersed in my understanding of this topic of experiential healing, I found some of his content too good to be true. I began to question the validity of what he was saying and despite this, decided to get up the next morning and begin the challenge.

The challenge is a simple one and easy to follow, but the depths to which you begin to understand your reality for me was quite unsettling. Each day you are told to answer specific questions about your life, people, experiences, feelings, and emotions. You journal your answers and post them in the group so everyone can see your

131

work. Now I guess for some being visible and vulnerable in itself is a challenge, I mean here I am writing and journaling my inner most thoughts and sharing them in the group with complete strangers on a Facebook group. I was reluctant at first but soon realised that this was a private group, and I didn't know anyone here, so I guess it felt safe to open up and share my feelings. Everyone was assured that at the end of the challenge the content would be removed, and the group closed so I had no reason not to trust this guy or the fact that my deepest thoughts and feelings might be shared around the globe. To be honest I was in such a deep hole at this time, this was the least of my worries. That night there was a live feed from Duke and his team, discussing the work that day and answering questions from people about the task they had taken part in. As I sat and listened to Duke and the questions from others, I became somewhat relieved to find that people were experiencing a similar set of emotions, issues in life and feelings about the five-day challenge. As a collective group of people, we were all there for a reason. Everyone had been drawn to the challenge in the face of personal grief, trauma or events that had happened in their life or they were experiencing in the moment.

I started to check out some of the other people in the group by searching their names on Facebook and it became clear to me that some of these folks were very spiritually aligned and practicing people in the world of healing and spirituality. Some were Reiki healers, light workers, tarot readers, meditation guides and all manner of different practices. This was all new to me and my first initial reaction was "these lot are a bunch of nutters", such was my scepticism about this kind of thing. But what kept me hooked was my connection to the group and visualisations I had always felt or experienced throughout my life, like the swans swimming in front of me in Scotland when seeking some guidance was just one example. I have over the years seen numbers, had inspiration on things that have often materialised in some way, connections and premonitions and events that can not be explained.

I felt instantly at ease with these people, and I continued to attend the live guided meditation which followed the Q & A. Inspired by what I was seeing and feelings I experienced when I took part in my first ever meditation, along with upwards of a few hundred other souls on this live was simply amazing. What happened next as I followed the guided meditation shook me beyond all comprehension. I was visualising parts and stories in my life that had you asked me a question about these events I could not have answered you, but as I was accessing the subconscious part on my mind and the clarity and understanding of these events were simply too real to ignore. I was accessing feelings and emotions and experiences from some forty years ago as a child and I was freaking out to be honest. At the end of the meditation, I was feeling tired and drained. I was puzzled and somewhat confused by the events that just happened and as I sat wondering what this all meant, I began to doubt this practise. I was in my head completely. I could not sleep that night at all. The realisations and clarity from the meditation kept me thinking all night. I was trying to understand the meaning of it all. Was it really happening? Was I in a dream state? Was I being brainwashed? was this a cult? I woke the next day and took on challenge two as instructed and journaled my thoughts and feelings on the topic. I had become quite emotional in doing so. I guess the previous night's meditation had opened the flood gates to further parts of my subconsciousness that had never been accessed before until now.

I posted the challenge and then asked a few questions on the Q &A post later that afternoon, hoping for some more clarity in a conscious state rather than in the depths of a guided meditation. That afternoon I spent much time googling things on spirituality, awakenings, and other forms of information in search of a further and deeper understanding of this world. The more posts I read and came across, the more confirmation I was getting that I was in fact on my own very real spiritual awakening. Now this to me was freaking me out big time. My understanding at this point and from the information that I had digested, was that not everyone experiences this awakening. If you do, it's normally as a result of something traumatic in your life and that the universe will only give this to people who have a purpose in life to help others on this path.

Now as I have stated many times in this book, I was not religious nor very spiritual nor interested in this kind of thing and was the biggest sceptic about all this kind of "woo-woo" stuff, but this was now a very real and tangible part of my life that I was experiencing in the real world and in this very moment. Day three challenge accepted. I journaled, posted, asked my questions, and waited for the live meditation that evening. After coming out of the guided mediation, I broke down in tears and cried for three hours continuously. I reached out to one of the team in this group as I was concerned about what was happening to me. I was assured it was all part of the process and perfectly normal and people would react to the meditation in different ways. My reaction was one of releasing suppressed emotions and was perfectly aligned to what I was feeling and going though. Despite the reassurances it still made for an uncomfortable three hours.

What was happening during this meditation was the release of suppressed feelings of abandonment that I was holding onto about my breakup with my first ever girlfriend. The feelings of abandonment by my mother, during my parent's separation and more recently the abandonment of my recent now ex-partner. Each one of those experiences happened in a similar way of me being cut out of these people's lives, through no choice of my own, and left to seek the closure very much on my own. I can say that evening I was spent, tired exhausted but felt much lighter. The clarity and the feelings of purging all these emotions made me feel completely at ease and accepting of these traumatic events that had happened in my life and I was finally able to accept them. Knowing and learning how I was emotionally attached to these situations and releasing the feelings of guilt, shame, and self-loathing, coupled with wanting to give love and wanting to be loved, was all the clarity I had been seeking to the way I was currently feeling.

Day four and five of the challenge followed a very similar path and structure and more things came to light as I followed this process. Feelings and emotions just popped up and showed themselves at the most bizarre timings "AHA" moments as Duke referred to them. Now by this point I was feeling so much better and positive, although still in my head about what was happening to me. I began to hear stories from other people's struggles which made mine a walk in the park in comparison. People had lost children in horrendous accidents or from crippling health conditions, people were sharing the traumas of sexual abuse and their journeys of self-destruction, with addiction to drugs, alcohol, sex, food, eating disorders - the list of suffering was endless and ranged from the mild to most severe traumas that most people could not comprehend. I began to see and hear about people releasing from these traumas, some people who had been in years of treatment for addiction, now for the first time, seeing the real root cause of their suffering from a subconscious and soul's perspective. People that were suffering from physical ailments and had done for years just like Duke, were reporting an easing of the pain almost instantly or within hours. Everyone in the group that was committed to this process were all sharing breakthrough moments about themselves and their lives. It would be fair and quite true to say this five-day challenge changed my life. At the end of day five, a zoom party was held by Duke and the team and we all got to see for the first time. These other brave souls face to face.

Up and to this point it was all just a profile picture and words but to now see my new friends was an amazing experience. Duke in this final live would often carry out an EH (experiential healing) process on someone live for all to see, to show everyone just what the process was and the techniques he has adapted over the years. Again, a deep guided meditation and specific guided questions to get to the route of the pain held in the subconscious part of the brain. It was amazing to see and watch in real time as the willing participant recalled a traumatic experience with a family member, which had for years caused so much pain and suffering. The release of her emotions was clear to witness, and I felt every part of her experience and journey to understand the suffering. Duke at the end of the evening invited those who wanted to sign up for his three-month course to contact one of the team the following day to discuss the content and fees for the course. As much as I wanted to do the course the fees were beyond reach at this time, so I declined but having seen the effects on me personally, I knew there was some validation and worth in what he was offering. The content of the five days remained visible for the following week allowing people to go back and revisit the notes, lives or the guided meditations should they want to access them again and seek further clarity that perhaps they had not got in the challenge. I recall that weekend being totally wiped out and did nothing that weekend. I could barely move such was the energy I had released that week. On Sunday evening just before going to bed, another post popped up on my Facebook feed and it was another free five-day challenge I signed up without any reluctance or preconceived idea of what it would entail.

This second challenge was by an ex-sniper from the military called James Boardman who had lost his identity when he left the forces. He too went into a downward spiral and lost relationships, his value, self-worth and purpose in life and so was running this course for men who were going through the challenges we all face. Now this course was a very different beast, it was aimed more at the physical and mental wellbeing for men by introducing routines and structure

137

back into their lives, motivation, and perseverance together with an element of fitness. Whilst I took the daily challenges and worked my way through the five days, I could not for some reason apply myself in the same way to the EH course.

The reason for this was that my life, at this point, did not have any structure in place. I wasn't working and my mind was still dealing with the fall out from the five days with Duke and the team on the EH challenge and I was finding it hard mentally to get that structure and routine in place for myself. My mind was still very much like a sponge - reading and taking in information from the spiritual journey I was now on, which I guess made it hard for me to focus fully on the course. I completed the course and again was offered to sign up for a twenty-eight-day challenge for a reasonable and fair fee. But as I had not been fully committed to the challenge, not through a want of trying, moreover in a mental capacity than anything else. I again declined to take the course as I did not see as much value in it for me based on my EH discoveries.

The following weeks I spent much of my time reading, which again is something I never used to do at all my evenings as for many years my evenings were spent watching T.V and relaxing after a day from work, something that used to frustrate my ex-partner immensely, that I later found out as one of the lame reasons for ending the relationship. I bought some books and spent hours reading and learning online, looking into this newfound part of my journey. I watched TED talks and listened to podcasts on every topic you could imagine. Within a few months I was completely immersed in this world of healing and spirituality to the extent that my life made complete sense and I had found a purpose. I began to see everything in front of me as clear as day. My patterns of behaviour, the reasons for my feelings and emotions and more importantly the same in others. Because of my own self-discovery, I was able to apply the same logic and thinking to that of my now ex-partner and decided to call her to tell her what I had been going through and most importantly to forgive her for the pain she had put me through. We exchanged words and I thanked her for what she had put me through and told her that I loved her regardless of the suffering and pain. She was somewhat surprised and confused at my explanation and pearls of wisdom and I think at some point she felt I was off my rocker. In some attempt to restore a connection with her I asked her to look at her own issues in the same light, but she instantly dismissed anything I had to say, saying she would deal with her stuff in her own way.

What I realised soon after this exchange, was that you cannot get people to change just because you have. The universe perhaps has not bestowed that blessing on the other people in my life and so they are not willing to take that difficult journey of self-discovery. Such was the clarity of my life at this point, I now had an answer to everything that had happened to me. My attachments to things, feelings, people, my beliefs around choices, circumstances and things changed as a result. I was seeing the world and my reality in a completely different way. There simply was not going back from this and to be honest, I wouldn't want to go back the old version of me - it sucked!

In June 2020, my daughter came to spend a night with me the first time since I was kicked out of home. Despite messaging her all this time, I had not physically seen her. I was excited but also nervous as to how she would see me know following the last three months of my journey. We sat down and chatted for a while as we caught up on things. She began to laugh a lot and I was surprised at this when I asked her why she couldn't stop laughing she said, "dad you've changed" Bingo! That was all the validation I needed to know that what I had being going through was the right thing and I was not losing my mind. She then proceeded to tell me that she hadn't seen me this happy in over three years! It was such a relief to know that the one person in my life that had always meant the most to me, was now back in my life and our connection had a chance of growing stronger than ever before.

I told her about my journey and what I had been up to and shared some pearls of wisdom from my newfound understanding. I also began to question her about her feelings and emotions about the events that had happened. It was perhaps my way of speaking my truth and coming from a different place now that I wanted her to be reassured that everything was fine and that her dad was now the dad, she always wanted me to be. For much of her childhood I was too wrapped up in my own guilt, shame, feeling a lack of self-worth and not being able to show her love or receive hers. Everything was on a different level now and she could see that for herself.

For the first time in my forty-seven years, I felt a true emotional connection to someone I loved with all my heart. Her acceptance of me was my comfort in all that had happened, and that all my pain and suffering was for a purpose and had meaning. I was now feeling at peace with everything in my life for the first time ever. We gradually spent more and more time together and she would come and stay with me often, each time I could sense she was becoming more at ease with me and that felt great to know that she felt comfortable around me again and moreover that she had her Dad back. As much as I was still feeling alone and isolated, I was now back at work, working from home and spending time with my closest friend again who I was also helping deal with some of his challenges. He is still facing his five year and daily battle from his divorce and separation, but he still doesn't have access to his twin girls now aged 10.

Our conversations with each other were honest, direct and nothing was held back, and he too, was amazed at my transformation and on occasions he would be amazed and somewhat puzzled at my knowledge and understanding of his events he was experiencing. "mate in all the years I have known you I have never heard you talk like this, where the fuck is all this coming from?" was his realisation of my transformation. I knew from the interactions with my daughter and my best friend I was now the person I should have been all along. My transformation in these last twelve months has been my biggest and most rewarding part of my life to date and I know my journey is in some way now only just starting. I have noticed in recent months just how many more people are speaking to me, know and seeking my guidance, friends and work colleagues are also seeing my transformation. Not only has my mind undergone this transformation but also my overall physical appearance has changed. I am eating better, exercising daily and generally taking better care of myself. Whilst I need to improve further this part of my transformation and there is still more work to be done its part of the journey.

My family have been very supportive over the last year and they have also noted my changes, conversations with them are somewhat questionable as they try to understand my new view on life and situations, but they all clearly know that whatever took place over the last few months has made a huge impact on me. And whilst I don't expect them to understand my journey or the events of the last twelve months, I am sure at some point they will get the understanding for themselves on some level. I also had a call out of the blue a few weeks ago from a friend I used to work with many years ago. I recall him sitting next to me in the office and he would be constantly talking about all things spiritual. He would listen to hours of podcasts from Eckhart Tolle and Sadhguru, much to my amusement and piss-taking. I had not a clue what the hell he was on about half the time, but now know that was him going through his spiritual awakening at the time and him reaching out to me during this time was perhaps his soul calling out to mine to offer some guidance and support and that some of us are divinely guided in life and are here to serve others.

What transpired on that call was three hours of discussion about the journey. It was a sign from the universe that him reaching out that evening was again validation and confirmation that I was on the right path now. We were discussing how to live life in the simplest of ways, to be content and happy and that material wealth and the trappings of success do not make you happy. We laughed and joked about living the life of a monk for pure enlightenment and divine guidance but agreed that was perhaps taking it to the extreme when we have the commitments that we both have in our current reality. We discussed the joys of spiritual guidance from the universe and all things divine. What transpired a few hours later, only confirms my connection to the universe and my understanding of this new world.

I thanked him for his valid contribution and words of great wisdom and went to bed feeling a little more grounded knowing that a dear friend was also on the same path as me. I picked up my read for the evening and began to read where I had left off the night before my book of choice was "Greenlights" by Matthew McConaughey, another enlightened soul, and a guy who too, has been divinely guided in life. I was reading the chapter about him taking off to a monastery in search of spiritual guidance where he asked one of the monks that he needed to speak to someone about his thoughts and feelings about what he was experiencing in his life. The monk in question turned to him and said you need to speak to "brother Christian". I nearly fell out of bed! I had just spent most of my evening talking about my life and seeking spiritual guidance from a friend and here was Matthew in his book doing the exact same thing with Brother Christian who shares the same name as me. (page 148) for those that want to check it out. I knew in this moment that it was another sure sign that I was divinely connected to god, spirit the universe. Seriously I cannot make this stuff up, even if I wanted to.

I emailed my friend and sent him a photograph of the passage in the book along with the photograph to validate my connection with the universe. We laughed together and felt it only correct that he now referred to me as Brother Christian and he would be referred to as brother Kevin, such was the resonance of that moment. As time rolls on and my journey continues, I am seeing and resonating with many more events such as the one just explained. My connection to this new world is now very real and very tangible to me and the resonance and witnessing such events only strengthened my belief in what I was experiencing and to some extent what I had felt all my life when seeing things, a sign of guidance from the universe.

CHAPTER 11.

REACHING OUT

A year had passed and despite my obvious growth in all aspects of my life, there was one facet that I was still holding on to all this time. I knew that despite the fact my relationship had ended and forced me to explore parts of me I never wanted to face, I wondered if my ex too had done the same work or faced her dark night of the soul. I had known from the brief and triggering conversations over the course of the year that she had not, such was the way she was still acting out when she called me, but I was hoping that perhaps with reflection and time, feelings and emotions may have changed between us.

I had found it difficult to respect her boundaries in the early months soon after the breakup but knew that I was in a much more grounded place now some twelve months on from the events that took place. I always said to myself that I would allow exactly one year to reach out again and establish if things could ever be worked out between us. I knew in my heart of hearts that I didn't want to feel this level of animosity towards her anymore and was kind of hoping that we could finally come together face to face and bring things to the correct closure for all concerned and from a place of love, rather than resentment and fear.

I knew with a new year fast approaching, I no longer wanted to hold onto this connection or feelings as I knew it was holding me back in life. Despite meditation and chord cutting to release these feelings for her even now I was struggling to release her. It was crunch time for me in finally making the conscious decision to let her go. I wrote her an honest and long letter detailing my beliefs about our relationship and my thoughts and feelings about how things were and how if she wanted to, we could grow together with my newfound wisdom.

Now I knew she was seeing someone else, and I knew my letter would be read as my communication always was. Despite not being able to talk with her she always read my letters or notes. The letter was sent, and I was relieved to have taken the step to finally see what would come of it. I knew the response would be short, sweet and to the point. I had an email back almost immediately saying that I needed to let it go now and move on with my life. Just as I had expected. My intuition was on point and that had she also done the inner work then us coming together to close the chapter from a place of love, would not have been an issue. Her short and direct response only confirmed she was still in her old mindset which was emotionally closed off and fearful of any interaction with me. I was at peace with this now and could finally commit to me and move forward. I could let her go, knowing that I had given it enough time and understanding to see who she really was. Still the same and devoid of all personal and emotional growth. As the saying goes "you can't teach an old dog new tricks "or "you can lead a horse to water, but you can't make it drink".

Me speaking my truth a year on and speaking from the heart space was my way of finally seeking closure to the breakup but there was one thing still bothering me and I knew it was the final door I needed to close before being fully free to moving on with my life as I had hung on far too long, but I knew it was part of my journey. In the recent visits by my daughter, I noticed that she was spending much of her time in her room chatting with friends on her phone and I sensed an air of reluctance about her to engage in conversation as we had done on previous visits. She was almost displaying signs of withholding her true feelings about something and I knew something was not right and despite my intuition I knew exactly what the issue was.

She messaged me the next week and asked if she could come and stay with me again, but I refused. She was somewhat unsure of my response. But I simply asked her to get her mum to call me as I needed to speak to her mum before she could come and stay again. Within minutes my ex was calling me to ask why my daughter was not able to stay. I simply asked my ex to be honest with me and tell me who she was now in a relationship with. Again, her refusal to answer my question and that it was none of my business fuelled another wave of abuse from her. I explained to her that she needed to speak her truth and that whatever she told me had not bearing on how I was feeling nor that it would cause me any more pain. The reason for her speaking her truth was the effect it was having on my daughter. I explained that she was again feeling uncomfortable

148

being with me and I told her that she was not engaging in conversation as she once did and that my daughter's reluctance to speak with me was because she was fully aware of my ex's new relationship and I could see my daughter was scared to let the cat out of the bag for fear of upsetting me. It was written all over her face every time I saw her and how she was showing up. She was living in fear of what she might say. Despite ten minutes of protest from my ex, I said either that she needed to come clean about who she was seeing, or my daughter could not stay with me as I didn't want her coming round to be with me, sitting there in fear or suppressing her feelings about the new relationship. I told my ex that what she was putting my daughter through emotionally was totally unfair and damaging.

Eventually she admitted her new relationship and I thanked her for being honest and said my daughter was welcome to come round at the weekend. I also asked her to tell me who he was although I knew anyway. I guess I just wanted to see how far I could push her to speak her truth. She carried on stating it was none of my business but said I had a right to know who this guy was as he was spending time with my daughter and as her father, I needed to make sure she was safe with him. Having undergone my healing and spiritual journey and just how I understood my ex from my own journey, I could not say that her choice of new partner considering her own history and mine did give me a genuine reason for concern.

She fed me all sorts of assurances that this guy was fine and a good man and that he too, had kids. It made no difference to me if he had kids or not, he could still be a complete nutcase and be a risk to my daughter based on his own patterns and beliefs and traumas. A point my ex again failed to accept or value. Such was her ignorance of the situation. I was finally at peace with the last 12 months.

My daughter arrived the next day and she was showing up completely differently now, we spent the whole evening together chatting, laughing, and talking all things spiritual - we had a right old laugh. She told me as much as she wanted to tell me about this new guy, and I did not push her for more truths I had no reason to. The fact she was now free to be herself, in my company, was all I needed to close that final door on this situation. The only final niggling confirmation I was seeking was what car he drove. My daughter said a white BMW. Penny Drop! I was spot on again with my intuition and feelings that my ex was having an affair behind my back. All her accusations of me lying and cheating on her and all the lame excuses she gave me for the breakup making out it was all my fault, was her projections about what she was doing. Yes, I had my issues, and I did things I was not proud of, but I was always honest about them and admitted my short comings and faced the consequences.

I simply cannot put a value on what this journey of spiritual awakening has done for me and level of understanding and clarity I now have in any given moment. I see right through people now and how they show up in front of me. It gives me the opportunity to read them and establish if they are genuine honest and fair people. My intuition can smell bullshit a mile away. I now know that should I decide to get involved with another relationship I will not be with just anyone. I can only be with someone that has been on a similar journey of spirituality and awakened enlightenment. I will know when that person shows up and I will know if it feels right.

I guess my previous choices, like most, are based on attraction and physical connection and shared values at the time of meeting. What I see now about my relationship with my ex is one of trauma bonding, attachments, and the need to feel unconditionally loved because neither of us were ever in a place to love ourselves first. What kept us together for so long, I guess, was physical attraction and a set of circumstances that connected us as that time, right place right time etc... and I guess for most that is how we meet our partners. I could say my ex was a karmic partner, even a twin flame partner in the realms of spirituality but looking at my life with her and the journey I have been on the dynamics of our relationship and the rollercoaster of ups and downs it would certainly confirm my belief in a twin flame partnership in the theoretical sense. The way we mirror each other and bring out the best and worst in each other only confirms this. All I can say is that she came into my life to teach me some lessons and those lessons have been truly guided and learned from. So, with all my love for her and blessings she has given me I wish her well on her journey. She deserves health, happiness, and peace I just wish she had found that in herself first, then perhaps I could have loved her how she has always wanted to be loved. I guess that goes for me too.

So, whilst the COVID-19 pandemic and the world has changed beyond all normality or how we have experienced it to this point, this pandemic and the breakup of my relationship have been the biggest blessings for me in my life. I was forced to face my "Dark night of the soul" and take the time out through circumstances, to inwardly explore who I am. I can say that for forty-seven years I felt I was living in a dark room and then someone has come in and switched the light on such was the realisation about who I am. Call it what you will or assign whatever meaning you want to it but "re birth" "enlightenment" "awakened" "re incarnation" all could be used to describe my soul at this moment in time. I now walk in life with gratitude for every experience I encounter. I realised that to be happy, I need to speak my truth and come from my heart space rather than the mind space and that in some small way everyone I meet will be a part of my journey and will be there for a reason.

I am aboard my "SOUL TRAIN". I am on the right track. I have a one-way ticket! and there is no going back. I will reach my destination even though I do not know where that is right now.

I can only live my life now in truth and honesty. I no longer fear judgements from others, and I have forgiven myself for all the wrongs I have caused others and for the wrong's others have caused me. I live for the moment I am worthy of love and acceptance and I know the universe has my back.

I now have an amazing group of friends that are my soul tribe and know that these amazing people will always be there in times of need. I am operating on a different vibration now and understand that I will only attract the right kind of people into my life from here on in. Those people who are not aligned with me will simply drop out of my life and I am ok with that. I don't seek validation from others anymore and I won't pretend to be someone I am not. I know exactly who I am, where I have been, where I have come from, and now for the first time I can now fully accept and love myself for the soul I am having a human experience!

"THE JUICE"

Realizations, patterns and limiting beliefs realized.

ENVIRONMENT

Although I recall very little if anything from my birth and time in Mexico it would be fair to say that my immediate surroundings were unfamiliar and not part of my genetic and ancestral timelines. Both my parents were in unfamiliar waters during my birth and so I guess were very conscious of this and adapted their emotions and feelings and my initial start in life to the unfamiliar surroundings. It is without doubt that this would have affected them on so many levels. Food, clothing, cultural differences would have all played a part on them and ultimately me from this early age. I cannot say with any certainty to what effect this shaped me as the person I am today but one feeling I have always felt was a fear of unfamiliar places or direction in life. From as early as I can recall I always wanted to know where and how I would get from point A to point B and I have always planned and navigated with deep thought about any direction in life however big or small the direction was that needed to be taken. Often procrastinating to such a degree, it consumes me mentally.

I always had reservations of unfamiliar places, people and situations and have never really been able to go with the flow. I can only assume this pattern of thought and behaviour was shaped during this time on the subconscious level.

As we progress through life our environment changes all the time, places, people, careers, family, and circumstances. We all strive for something with an element of stability which stems from the ego's desire to keep us safe. Generations and ancestral timelines and years of social programming convince us that to feel safe, our environment needs to offer some sort of protection. We look for people to love us, to care for us, to support us, to need us, to rely on us and we expect that to be reciprocated.

The home is probably considered by most, to be the most stable and safe place to be. As a child it offers (in most cases) that protection. Our parents ensure we are fed, watered, clothed, have a place to shelter from the elements and harsh reality of the world. Once in this environment we adapt to life within it and form understandings and beliefs of what that means to us, we form opinions and judgements and attach meanings to what is a safe place. Sadly, for some the home environment is not a safe place and is easily the place where we feel our most vulnerable too. Seeing parents fight or argue, get punished for being disrespectful by parents, the stress to feed us, clothe us and raise a family, the costs, the bills, the constant worry that it could be lost at any moment if made redundant or we fall ill, unable to work.

Any perceived or real threat that compromises the home or this safe environment that we attach to, is a fear we all feel daily subconsciously. Whilst in my relationship, I also had the belief and desire to provide this for my family and my partner. My pursuit to match the expectations of my childhood trappings of the home environment were always a constant sense of burden. When I was out of work or unable to meet the bills, that environment of safety that we all attach to was always threatened, my ability to provide was questioned by my partner, resentment became a real issue and I always caused a deep-seated feeling of lack within me and whether

I could achieve this safe and protective environment for my own family.

For me, the home was my safe-haven, and I guess because of my childhood condition allowed me to feel safer than most, stepping away from this security was always a fear or felt uncomfortable a pattern and subconscious belief now realized. My home was also the place where me and my partner had many disagreements and arguments which tainted that idyllic dream of safe place for us both and for the kids. It was also the place of some very fond and happy times too. Such was the drama in the house at times, it wasn't a surprise that my stepson decided when he finished school to go and live with his dad for the first time in seventeen years.

The arguments that happened between us, triggered in me all that I had experienced as a child and with my parents, and certainly the day my mum walked out of the home. Any opportunity I had to avoid confrontation I would often leave the family home to seek some peace and get away from the drama. I hated every single experience that caused these moments and regret them all, but such was my programming and my partner's, neither of us had the clarity to resolve these in a loving and respectful way. Neither of us had that safe peaceful, loving, nurturing, environment, and both of us subconsciously acted this out in our own relationship with negative programmes based on past hurts. Being thrown out of my home after seventeen years of family life was heart breaking not only for me but for my daughter too.

My daughter had witnessed that very thing. I did everything I could to avoid following my own experience with my parents. I now know and understand every emotion my daughter will now face because of that night. The sad truth is that I am the only one who can see this damage this will cause for my daughter later in life as my ex is still very much asleep in every sense of the word.

My Awakening has confirmed to me on many levels that I do not need that big house anymore. I do not strive for material wealth or that environment, the flash car, the largest state of the art TV money can buy, the clothes, the labels, none of it is relevant or valued in my life anymore. I do not need those things and I will live within my means from now on. Having spent years battling to seek that socially acceptable media portrayal and appearance of what success and happiness is, it no longer serves me any value. I have a modest home that I do not own, I have no ties to it, and I can choose my own destiny and change my environment should I feel the need to.

It is not just the home environment that I see differently now, it's also people in my life. As this journey has unfolded, I have had to release and let go of people that I held in my life for seventeen years whilst in my relationship. Some of them family, some of them friends. Gladly some of these people were contributing factors to my suffering during my relationship and I am glad and happy that they will no longer hold influence over my life or my happiness anymore. Those people in my life that were distant from me for all this time I am slowly rebuilding those bridges again and reconnecting with people who have mattered to me the most, but because of my suffering I distanced myself from them. The biggest part of my environment that has changed for me is just how many amazing loving and supportive people I have in my life that I could count on if needed at the drop of a hat. My "SOUL TRIBE". These people who have held space for me over the last twelve months. They have listened to me be completely open about my feelings and emotions, they have never judged me for my wrongs, and they have all loved me unconditionally. I feel so blessed and privileged to have this tribe around me on my journey and they all know who they are. There are simply too many of them to list. But I love each one of them.

So, if you are not happy with your environment take some steps to change it. Move home, get out of that relationship that is sucking your soul dry, let go of that job that's not fulling you anymore. Lose that group of friends or family that do not value you or the choices you have made or cannot accept who you are. The only person that can change your environment is **YOU!** Sometimes our environment is changed for us and we can do nothing but accept that, like in my case. I now take with me that fact that as devastating as it was, it was not my partner who changed it, or me that changed it, but the universe stepping in to get me to where I am now. I would not be on this path, nor writing this book had I not been guided in some way.

"Changing yourself to fit into your environment can be an act that serves you or destroys you. Know what you are changing into"

Shamala Tan

APPROVAL

I guess another self-limiting pattern realised, was that my dad had always been the provider and I guess I looked up to him in that way. I was always striving to replicate his success and experiences in my own life and always felt a lack of self-worth if I stumbled to meet his level of achievement in my own existence. The biggest realisation following my awakening was a fear of his approval on the subconscious level never fully realised until now.

Such was the love for my dad and all the material wealth that surrounded me as a child growing up, I guess I set the belief that to feel fulfilled in my own life, I would need to match this achievement if not for my own self worth but also for his approval on some level. Now I know parents will always approve of their kids, whether achieving or not in life, but that still doesn't take away the fact that we often look up to our parents as role models and have these attachments.

Approval and being accepted for who we are is the driver in many relationships and acceptance of self. We seek our parent's approval, we seek the approval of our partners, wives, girlfriends, family, friends, and our even own children, not to mention the boss who pays our wages. Since my awakening the only approval I now need is my own. Every time I lost someone I loved or cared for in a relationship I saw that as a form of rejection and refusal to approve of who I was to that person.

I was always seeking approval from that person that I was loveable, accepted, wanted, and needed. The minute I felt my partner disapprove of who I was, or she could no longer accept me for the person I had become, I began to question my value, my worth and if I were needed or wanted. This led to years of depression, confusion, worry and battles in my own mind. I guess my partner felt the same way also. Our patterns and programmes had both guided us to a set of expectations from each other based on social conditioning, past experiences and values that were never fully realized or aligned, and certainly never openly discussed.

There was only one way the relationship was going to go. I know writing this book has also questioned my feelings and emotions about approval and the fear of it. What if my parents read this, will they still approve of me? what will my ex-partner think? what will my friends or work colleagues think? will they approve of me after this? will my daughter still approve of her dad, was the biggest fear. After some reflecting on this, I decided it really did not matter what these people think of me. I am not seeking their approval anymore as this is my approval of me.

Social programming is today the biggest issue on the planet facing everyone. Our children are fed all kinds of shit via Instagram, tiktok, twitter and all these other media channels, that to feel accepted and approved of in society you need to have material wealth, designer clothes, look a certain way or live a certain way of life. We are constantly fed this shit daily to feel approval. The government and the so-called political figures that run our countries are telling us we must follow the rules to be approved of in society. Covid has highlighted this issue more so than ever, controlling "nanny state" that ensures everyone must comply with what others tell us to do.

You do not need anyone's approval but your own, no one can tell you what to do with your life and no one has the right to either.

"Those who's approval you seek the most give you the least"

LifeHack Quotes

GIVING & RECEIVING LOVE

Another programme was one of receiving love from my parents. As my mum was the main care giver as a child, as most mums are, I was always able to accept and receive this love from my mum. My dad was always working twenty-four seven and I guess I felt somewhat short-changed in receiving his love as he was not around for much of the time. There was an imbalance of love given and therefore my subconscious mind believed on some level the only way for me to receive love was from my mum or a female of significance importance in my life. I know both parents loved me deeply and still do, but only receiving that love from one parent, in my opinion, causes the imbalance in children and is the catalyst for the imbalanced beliefs we form in our minds. We will naturally gravitate and attach to the one that provides the most, love comfort and safety.

This attachment caused issues for me later in life such was that attachment to receiving that love from the female on a subconscious level. As I have stated the only way I felt love in intimate relationships was through physical intimacy. I was always seeking and happy to receive and give this love in the physical form. My partner was the opposite. Always fearful of hugs and closeness and never showed any outward displays of affection in public. She always used to say I am not that kind of person "I don't do hugs" and laughed it off all the time. Even to this day she shows very little

163

affection to friends, family or even her own kids in the physical sense. I can only assume this stems from her own traumas from childhood and knowing her mum and dad neither of them are very affectionate people. So, I guess that was her programming, one I battled with all the time.

There are many documented understandings of love languages and I guess not knowing your own type makes it difficult to see others. Perhaps if we both understood these love languages our story would have been very different. I can see now, just how much both our childhood experiences and programming affected our ability to come together in a loving place. There was love between us and at times an immense feeling of love between us, but not being willing to express that or receive it made it a constant battle of wills. I suppose such was the rollercoaster of emotions between us, and the layers of resentment and mistrust over time that had built up, we both stopped giving and receiving love to ourselves.

We would always put the other first in this regard and kept doing all we could to show that love towards each other at the expense of our own self-love. I will be totally honest and say that I was not very loving to myself, and the feelings that I was not able to show my love in a way that my partner could accept or value which made me very despondent. I was always my biggest critic, which often led to spells of deep depression and frustration. I am sure my partner also felt this way.

I realise that my way of giving love was always in the physical sense rather than from an emotional stance. It was the only way I knew how to show love for someone and with my experiences over time with the women in my life, it only rooted that in my subconscious as the only way to give love. For some, showing and receiving love is in the form of material things and material wealth, for others it's intimacy and for some it's just being present and being there for others. Irrespective of how, when, and why you show or give love, you first need to give that to yourself. If you don't have the capacity to love yourself for who you are, you are never going to be in a place to give or receive that with others. Healing past traumas accepting and letting suppressed feelings and emotions go, instantly and naturally brings you to a place of balance and unconditional love. When we heal the past and accept the lessons, we simply learn to come from the heart space and love and accept unconditionally.

"To give and receive love you have to be in touch with pain, you have to be capable of provoking it and feeling it".

Jeanne Morea

FEARFUL AVOIDANCE

Because of my medical condition, throughout most of my childhood, I was always avoidant at getting close to people. I was always content and happy never really stepping forward in life or drawing attention to myself. Always happy to sit at the back of the class, avoiding friends and felt quite comfortable in my own company. As my condition cleared up, much of my patterns and subconscious beliefs surrounding this aspect of my life had already been cemented in my mind. Looking back now I can see that even in work situations, I would feel more comfortable working independently whenever possible. Although working with teams of people I would always still try and remain as independent as possible.

This was also a trait my dad had, having spent most of his life self-employed so again, me mirroring this aspect too. I recall asking my daughter when she came to stay with me a question "What do you remember about me and mum when we were together?" what one thing stood out for you?" Her answer flawed me "you and mum were never in the same room". Now this hit me hard and again, confirmed my conditioning over all these years and through my childhood as I recall spending time with my grandparents on many occasions.

My nan used to sit in her room watching old films and knitting for England and my grandad would sit in his room and watch snooker on a black and white television or listen the radio. There was a door which separated these two rooms and often my nan would slam the door shut to ignore my grandad and his jovial antics. My younger brother would often be in the room with my grandad, and I would be in the room with my nan. I grew up surrounded with the belief and experience that separation was acceptable in some way. My parents did it all the time when my dad was working at home, I experienced this environment with my grandparents, and it was apparent in my own relationship. Like I have stressed all along, the subtlety of these experiences manifest themselves so deeply on the subconscious you really have no idea you are living in this un-awakened state. This I guess, made it difficult for people to get close to me on some level and that was also witnessed in intimate relationships too. I never felt able to fully engage with the people around me or in social circles, except for very close and trusted friends and family. As I look back now the fear I felt and shared with my partner when attending the many gigs and rock concerts surround by hundreds of people, I guess stems from this point in my life. It also explains my love of wide-open spaces and nature, where I do not feel so closed in by my surroundings. I can clearly see just how much this part of my life has affected me and limited my life experiences to date. It also shows me just how much this thought, or belief has ruled over my life and for so long.

This behaviour of avoidance would also explain why even now, as I sit here and write this, I have a very small and very limited circle of friends or ones I could call on if needed. I have friends all over the globe, both male and female and have made some great friends because of this journey. Whilst COVID is rife and most of the world is unable to see our friends and family, I can see the friends that I have, I have not seen or made the effort with for some time.

167

Looking back on my relationship with my ex-partner I can see that for every day of the years we were together, I was by her side in one way or another, (just not in the same room). She would often question me as to why I never made plans or spent time with friends, and, again, this confirms to me that she was able to see this in me, but I refused to see it. I was, by default, living in my subconscious and programmed mind space all this time. It saddens me to think just how much I have held back from because of this programming. I guess it is all too easy to make up some excuse not to spend time with friends and family and we all do, but to truly see the reason for this behaviour and where it comes from is without a doubt lifechanging.

I can see clearly now how my ex-partner was also a fearful avoidant to some degree. Her lack of wanting to get close to me and being more content spending time with friends and being in social settings was always her programme. Couple this with the lack of her emotional availability that stems from her programmes in childhood and past experiences. Both of us were complete opposites when it came to connecting with each other in the emotional sense. Her emotional unavailability in the relationship for me was the biggest battle. How could I love someone who had probably never experienced love in her own life? Her reluctance to be emotionally vulnerable, I can see stems from her early teenage years when faced with experiences with her mother and past relationships. She became fiercely independent and stepped away from those she loved relaying on her own ability to deal with emotional matters. Suppressing these feelings and never being around anyone she felt safe enough with to release these with. I feel that because of my own avoidance issues, she felt uncomfortable to be open with me.

Every relationship, either family, friends or loved ones will give us both good and bad experiences. We naturally form judgements about those experiences and programme the mind to either reject or accept people in our lives based on these experiences. Many people who have had damaging relationships are, by default, fearful of getting close to someone again for the fear of going through the pain again should it all go south. Each time we are setting ourselves up and self-sabotaging ourselves to fail in relationships because of past experiences. You often hear women say, "I always attract the same type of bloke". Well, the chances are that you have somewhere in your childhood an experience or a relationship trauma with a male figure in your life that you have not accepted or healed from, and by default have an attachment to the same kind of bloke each time. The same was for me and my attachment to the female. Only when you explore your past can you see the changes you need to make for a better choice for a partner moving forward.

Whoever you meet on your path, promise me one thing, that whoever you are with, please live in the moment with that person. Do not fear what might happen, do not fear what could happen, do not fear what you are or not bringing to the relationship. Do not fear or avoid intimacy, do not avoid the pain, do not avoid the hard conversations, and do not fear or avoid being vulnerable with that person.

But do heal from your past pain first!

Despite the longing to be in another relationship as soon as possible, such was the void I knew and felt again, this time everything had to be different for me. My spiritual awakening gave me the clarity I needed not to pursue anyone and focus completely on my own healing and journey. I had to finally put an end to the repeating and cyclical patterns of my past and to change the direction of my life once and for all. I know that my next relationship will not be one born from one of attachments but from a place of truth, honesty, and unconditional love for that person. Added to that, I now have this book as my dating CV if you will. A point of reference for my partner to understand who and what I truly am. If they can accept this book and see the value in it, then I guess they will accept and see that value in me.

ACCEPTANCE

For me, although I was accepted by my parents and a few close friends throughout my childhood and early teens I cannot help but now reflect on my life and throughout this journey and see that I did not feel fully accepted. Again, this was my own belief held in my mind that I was not good enough. I was not accepted as a child because of my fearful avoidance programming and did not reach out to seek that acceptance from others. I did not feel accepted by my dad as I was not able to match or live up to what he had achieved in life and I guess what I thought were his expectations of me.

I did not feel accepted in school due to my lack lustre ability to perform in the lessons of basic academic grounding. I did not feel accepted by my mum because of my condition and the stress it was causing her for all the years we battled with it. I felt in some way to blame for her having to give unconditionally to me during this time and had I not had this issue then I guess she would have been more accepting of me. But I guess the biggest realizations was that I was not accepting myself and who I was growing up. I always felt different to the others, not as social, not as clever, not as friendly, not as approachable as the other kids.

As we enter relationships, we often put our best foot forward in the beginning. We always show our best and most accepted characteristics and personality traits that we know are positive aspects of ourselves and have been accepted in the past. Rarely do we start relationships exposing our flaws, weaknesses and struggles as we perceive and believe if we do show this level of vulnerability and emotion, we will automatically be rejected on some level and will not get that acceptance. The ego steps in and calls upon all the positive aspects of ourselves to ensure we get that acceptance from others.

On my journey I have accepted that to be truly accepted by others you first must accept yourself, even the bad or dark aspects of who we are. Only when you accept these can people accept you too. If you can come from a place of total acceptance within, will you naturally begin to feel accepted by others. I would like to think that we all have that one close friend in our lives that knows who we really are. The friend that knows your battles, the friend who accepts you fully, the friend that is always there for you in times of need and the acceptance with that friend is reciprocal without judgements or attachments.

In my relationship with my ex-partner, I accepted from day one that I was prepared to fully accept her on every level, and I guess she felt the same. The problems appear and cracks begin to show when we start to see the flaws in someone, the weakness, the behaviours in these intimate partners. That is when the acceptance of these issues becomes increasingly hard to overlook, accept or value in our lives. The love is there but the judgements and mistrust creep in, based on our own values of what is deemed acceptable to us, which is the programming from our past, and no two people will ever be the same in this regard. Inevitably these differences and truths will cause doubts, fears and questions that we now find ourselves having to deal with. What are we willing to overlook? what are we able to accept in someone else? what does, accepting these aspects of someone else mean about us?

Obviously, we are all attracted to the best aspects of people, some of it is genetically embedded in our DNA through ancestral timelines as to the kind of person we will accept and much of it is through conscious choice. So much of our choice to be with someone is based on acceptance of social conditioning and aesthetics. We know what we are attracted to physically and what we are not. We know that we are seeking someone who can provide for us on every level sexually emotionally spiritually etc. and that is perhaps why we often make mistakes time and time again with our choices. We only accept those who we feel can tick all the boxes.

Everyone has freewill to choose who they want in a partner or relationship, but I now make no judgements about anyone's choice. But the simple fact is that no one person can give you everything you seek in a partner. To be happy in a relationship it is my belief that you will have to compromise on some level and be accepting of peoples flaws and weaknesses.

For me to accept someone in my life I need to know they have healed from the past, that they too, have been on a journey like mine. They can accept weaknesses in others and flaws and are not seeking the "ONE" because the reality of it is that is no such thing. My values are now one of honesty, authenticity, vulnerability and emotional openness and truth. I do not care how much money or wealth you have. I am not interested in the big-ticket items or living up to the socially accepted norm of what life should be or how it is portrayed. I want to be with someone who will accept me for who I

173

am today. I have been to hell and back and battled to accept myself on this journey the least you can do is also accept me as I am in the present moment.

"The art of acceptance is the art of making someone who has just done you a small favour wish that he might of have done you a greater one".

Martin Luther King

SHAME & GUILT

I felt a huge amount of shame and guilt throughout my childhood and early teens due to my condition. The shame I felt was for myself that I should not be having these issues. I was ashamed of myself for this limiting condition and even though my parents did everything they could to make it acceptable and ok for me, I still can't help the fact that I felt ashamed because of it. Despite years of treatment and assessments, the doctors couldn't find anything physically wrong with me which would have presented itself as a diagnosable and treatable condition. I recall now that the doctors felt it was a psychological disorder and perhaps that was the reason my mum tried hypnosis as a last resort.

It would certainly explain now the realisations of, some 35 years later, manifested itself in my psyche, my patterns and my behaviour during my life and choices I made. It also goes to prove that during this spiritual awakening and exploring my subconscious mind for clues, this one thing stands out the most prolific but was the last to be realised. The feelings of guilt during this time I guess was the effort and time my parents spent trying to make this ok for me. Had I not had the condition would the stress of this on them been less and would things have been different for all of us as a family? I cannot help but think that this stress in some way, because of this situation, contributed to the dynamics of my parent's relationship. Whilst I know both my parents would not agree with this statement at all, the guilt I held on to subconsciously for all these years perhaps why I took their breakup so hard, and that at some point I felt partly to blame.

Throughout my relationship with my ex-partner, I felt an equal amount of shame and guilt for not living up to the social norms of what a family life should be in the eyes of the world. My guilt over job moves, money issues and being emotionally stable for my family, being the provider, the main breadwinner, the stepdad I should have been to my stepson, the dad my daughter needed in her earlier years, the pain and hurt I caused my ex-partner when I looked outside the relationship because I did not feel loved or wanted by her. I can see now that whilst I know where I have gone wrong in all this and know exactly the reasons for my choices, it goes without saying that she equally had issues to deal with, which I can clearly see in her now. It would have made no difference to our relationship had anything been any different. It simply was never going to work based on our patterns and programmes. I guess the saying is true "only when you step back from something can you see the real truth". If I had not loved her as deeply as I did, then my spiritual awakening and realisations and the last twelve months would not have happened with the intensity that they have.

I am so grateful for the pain and hurt I went through over this separation. I have released shame and guilt about my seventeen years with her and what went down between us. I know that I will always love her for giving me this opportunity to find myself and to be there for my daughter moving forward. I will always love her for giving me my daughter, who I now have back in my life and a connection I could only dream of with her.

I have a much stronger and emotional appreciation for my parents and what they mean to me and what they have given me in life. Despite the adversities we went through as a family, I know they did all they could with what they had and knew from their past and childhood patterns and programmes. They too had no choice but to do what they did, it was all in the subconscious mind for them too. I want them to know that they should not feel any guilt or shame for the choices they made or for the hurt and pain they caused me at times throughout my life. I accept it all and have so much love for them that it has brought me to this place I now find myself in.

"Shame needs three things to grow exponentially in our lives: secrecy, silence, and judgement"

Brene Brown

"Guilt is rooted in actions of the past, perpetuated in the lack of action in the present, and delivered in the future in pain and suffering"

David Roppo

ATTACHMENTS

I formed many attachments in my life, and I guess it ties in with acceptance of self and by others. Feelings of isolation I felt as a child because of my perceived issues, coupled with my early sexual emotional discoveries, I feel these created an attachment to my physical sexual connections. My perceived thoughts and feelings of acceptance or lack of, was only really diminished by me seeking self-gratification through sexual arousal. Whether that was on my own or with someone else. For me it was acceptance of self when I could not achieve that sense of acceptance through normal situations or circumstances.

When I started having intimate relationships with the women on my journey, the feelings of acceptance were heightened to atmospheric levels. Sexual intimacy was not only providing me with the feelings of gratification and self-acceptance, but also acceptance from the female which up and to my late teens I had always doubted. Coupled with the fear of never having a girlfriend because of who I believed I was, and because of my condition. just made this attachment even more addictive.

Having spent most of my pubescent testosterone fuelled youth with my female teenage friend instead of male counterparts, strengthened my attachment to the fairer sex. I was soon attached to the idea that feelings of love and acceptance was as a direct result of sexual intimate relationships. Now on some level that is the same for everyone to a degree. When we are sexually intimate with someone there are a release of chemicals in the brain that give that endorphin rush and the feeling of being in love.

The realisation through my awakening about this, was that I was only feeling loved and accepted when having this experience, such was the programme and beliefs I held around this part of my life. My understanding of what it felt to be loved and accepted was 90 % of the time based purely on sexual intimacy. Such was the attachment to this situation I was not able to receive that love from my partner unless it was through physical intimacy. I was purely attached to the physical part of my relationship to feel accepted. With age, health and physical changes in my partner also complicating the desire for this from her side, I guess my selfish and relentless pursuit in seeking this, pushed her further away and made us both questioned our own worth and value in the relationship. The abandonment I felt from my mum and then first ever girlfriend when they both left without explanation created an even stronger attachment to the females in my life subconsciously more than I had ever thought. I know also that my ex-partner has abandonment issues from her parent's separations and then four failed relationships. The patterns of attachment and co-dependency are clear to see and very real for most.

I was also attached to the idea of money and material wealth, but because my internal lack of self, I was not able to fully meet that objective in life which also caused much frustration and suffering in my mind. The attachment to living up to my father's success story was always in my thought as his eldest son. I think on some level, all men tend to follow in their father's footsteps to some degree.

Whether that shows up in a family perspective, relationship dynamic or choice of career paths. I also think women may have the same calling to assimilate with their mums. Again, social programming that we are all led to believe will fulfil us.

I was attached to the idea that, as the man of the house, I should be the strong, dependable, secure and the protector. The reality of this was far from the truth in my mind. I put my ex-partner on a pedestal from day one and lived in her shadow for seventeen years such was my attachment to her. She was the strong, stable, financially secure and the dependable one, but because of that, I was never able to grow with her, she was always one step ahead on that front.

I guess the dynamics of our relationship were opposites. She was the mainstay of the home and I was the more nurturing and homemaker. I guess my early days in the hotel and catering business and time spent serving others, was a role that I felt at ease with and comfortable with.   Spiritually my ex-partner is certainly in her masculine energy and I am very much in my feminine energy and I guess the reason for our conflicting dynamics of our relationship in the physical reality.   Had I known earlier about these energy dynamics in this sense I perhaps could have used this to our benefit but all it did cause was confusion and issues.

"Attachments lead to expectations and expectations lead to disappointments".

"The route of suffering is attachment, look within. Be still". Buddah

CURIOUSTY & DENIAL

My heady bachelor days with multiple partners of varying degrees of sexual experiences meant I always had a curious nature regards to sexual matters. All my sexual experiences up and to the point I met my ex-partner had formed a belief and pattern of behaviour that I carried into that relationship, with the expectation that my partner would share my enthusiasm and passion for sexual fulfilment and exploration. Now every man who is in a loving, connected, and intimate relationship wants to have regular sexual encounters with the woman he loves, for it to be passionate and sensual in equal measures and I am no different on that front. I guess my inability to share openly my wants and needs, not to mention my experiences to date with the woman I wanted to spend the rest of my life with was probably my biggest downfall. It was also my biggest fear that had I shared this with her, I was fearful of losing her and her acceptance and most importantly her love for me. I guess the fact that I was not fulfilling her needs on many other levels, emotional financial, family life etc. because of my many other programmes and beliefs this made this virtually a no-go area for me to discuss with her. It was easier to live out my curiosities online and live-in complete denial. Do not get me wrong, there are many patterns and behaviours I now see in my partner that also caused intimacy issues between us, so although we are both guilty of living with the programmes in our subconscious minds - this was my issue alone and one, that I wish I had this level of clarity on years ago.

Her use of alcohol was and still is, in my opinion, her biggest issue. Her father tradesman by profession and musician the rest of the time, meant I guess she saw her dad growing up and still does down the pub most evenings. If you ever wanted to know where he was, chances are he would be down the boozer. My ex-partner often used to say she takes after her dad and has always been a drinker. The night we went out with my mates and she nailed us all on tequila should have been a warning sign of things to come. But like most, it was all part of the experience at that time. Sadly, the partying and going out drinking has never stopped or showed any signs of slowing down and despite several discussions to tell her drinking, was causing me some concerns not only for her health but our intimate relationship, not to mention the fights and what the kids witnessed at times. She had made no attempt to see it other than a fact of life and something she was prepared to do nothing about. I guess this was her attachment issue and was also in denial, such was her need to fill that emotional void within.

It should not come as any surprise to you, having read this book that both of us were doing things to avoid the inner pain and the voids we were feeling during our relationship and both found something to deal with those feelings of emptiness. It pains me to see it now the reasons behind it and just how simple it would have been to have resolved these issues and knock this shit on the head so we could have come together from a genuine and loving place. I guess for some people dealing with the root cause of the issue is far harder to face than the addictive and avoiding behaviour itself.

It is scientifically proven and documented that any form of addictive behaviour is linked to an emotional trigger in the mind and stems from a time of emotional trauma. We were both defensive about our own behaviours and were both in denial about it.

"Defensiveness often reveals an area of our lives where we're in denial".

Kyle Idelman

RESPONSIBILITES

For most, the first time we become responsible for our own existence would be when we go to university or step way from the family home. Our parents are always in the background to support and always will be but learning to be independent is a big step. At this point in life, you make your own decisions, stand on your own two feet and really get a sense of who you are.

My ex-partner had taken that step from a very early age in her late teens but for me it was in my early twenty's. I cannot help but think that late start for me compared to my partners, obviously showed up in behaviours and decisions I made whilst in the relationship with her. The fact that I returned home to support my dad and my brother when my mum left gave me a set of responsibilities I should never have had to face at a time when I should have been living independently and making my own life choices rather than worrying about my home life and those still in it.

I guess I was again seeking approval from my dad, by choosing to step up in this way, but always feeling guilty for myself for not making a different choice and going it alone sooner. For my ex-partner, having left home at an early age she was the complete opposite. She was fiercely independent and did whatever it took to succeed in life. Do not get me wrong, that was one of her qualities which I loved about her and still is to this day, she is the same. The downside to that experience was that I guess she was not shown love and support by her parents when she should have perhaps needed it the most. Like me to some degree, she felt the loss of her parents during separation and associated the lack of love and acceptance and ultimately rejection as something painful and emotionally traumatic and therefore closed up emotionally. Unable to let anyone get too close for fear of having the hurt and pain show up again.

Not having to rely on anyone else is a great strength to have and one we should all strive for that self-independence. We all know that the only person you can truly rely on is yourself at the end of the day. My responsibilities all changed when I met my stepson for the first time and knew I would have a bigger responsibility than most. Taking on someone else's child is a huge responsibility and at the time I thought long and hard if I made the right choice in getting into the relationship with her. I love my stepson and despite our difficult and troubled relationship, at times often influenced by other family members, I am proud to say he is now a young man of this world, working hard and earning a small fortune. A small part of me smiles knowing that I had an influence on his life for the better and that who he is now, is partly down to me. I always wanted a family and never at any point did I question just how much it would mean to me. The only thing I questioned and battled with, was myself to be able to provide for mine as my parents did for me. I did succeed as I have a daughter who is a chip of the old block and a stepson, I am proud to call my stepson. Although I no longer have the responsibility of a family in the traditional sense anymore, I still have a responsibility to my daughter and more importantly myself.

I may not have the material wealth, a big home cars etc... but my daughter will grow up knowing her dad has changed his life around and has all the tools he now needs to be the best version of himself. She can see where I have been, how far I have fallen and how well I got back up from adversity and that for me is perhaps my greatest responsibility to her knowing just what it takes to get back up and be authentic.

This book is my responsibility to her, allowing her to see who I am. This is my legacy to her, and I feel it is the greatest gift any father can give their kids. For my daughter to see who her dad is on a soul level, to see the mistakes he made and to see how choices influenced him on every level, and because of the ancestral patterns and programmes he was subconsciously living with. For her to have this understanding to live in her truth will guide her on the right path in this journey.

"It's only when your take responsibility for your life, that you discover how powerful you are?"

Alannah Hunt

FAMILY SEPARATION

Having witnessed my parent's battles throughout the years as many do growing up, I can count the many stressful situations that played out before me. My dad's choice to go self-employed, risking the family home at times while setting up and running his own business. The fights over money and stability, the highs and lows. I had no idea just how these events would shape and mould my subconscious mind and then play out in my own reality years down the line.

The feelings of abandonment when my mum left, were clearly deeper rooted than I could have comprehended or realised. Also, the events that followed which ultimately determined my own path. Witnessing my family falling apart caused me to overcompensate in my own family and to do everything I could not to repeat the same fate. I guess clinging onto the belief and want to succeed subconsciously caused other issues in my relationship. I have pretty much mirrored my father's story with my mum and can see all the faults in my own life play out as I reflect on my life.

My ex-partner had also experienced family separation with her parents although at a much younger age. The effects at whatever age are equally damaging and should never be overlooked. Her mother went on to have multiple failed relationships and so too, did my dad. My mum managed to have a long-term relationship and so too did my ex-partner's father. The dichotomies and dynamics of these circumstances simply cannot be ignored. It is all programming, and no one is exempt from it or the problems it causes in our own lives. I appeal to anyone who has suffered a separation break up or divorce to seriously go back to this time and re-live the experience again in your own mind. Be ok with it, accept it and be ok with the emotions and feelings you felt at that time. Give yourself and the inner child within you, the love that you wanted, needed, and deserved when your world was falling apart. Cry like a baby if it helps, it did me. Show your emotions, be vulnerable and accept yourself for allowing to feel this pain.

Now I am not advocating to stay in relationships that are clearly damaging, abusive or toxic. You will know in yourself by having read this book if your relationship is worth saving or not. Unfortunately, many people reading this book will be in a similar position to me and having missed the opportunity to repair these programmes and patterns and to be with the person they just wanted to love. I honestly believe that no relationship has to end. I would love to see the divorce figures drop rather than increase exponentially every year as they do, but unless couples can deal with the traumas from childhood, the patterns and programmes within our subconscious mind and deal and accept ourselves and each other from a place of unconditional love and acceptance, I don't see this dynamic changing any time soon.

What I do see is that the world is slowly waking up to being more authentic and living more consciously than ever before, there seems to be an ever-increasing desire to make the world a better place. Even if one couple resonates with anything in this book and I have saved a family from separation or divorce then my work is done. If you are on your own, learn to live by yourself first and do the healing and the inner work so that you are in the right place to ensure your

189

next relationship has a chance of being everything you dreamed it would be. Break those patterns, programmes, and beliefs you have held onto and let go of all the stories you told yourself about what the perfect relationship should be or look like. Also accept the fact that you might not ever been in a relationship again and that too is OK.

"Separation is not the end of love; it creates love". Nancy Friday

SELF-WORTH

I was beginning to question my value in life and my own self-worth. Why does this keep happening? why is it only happening to me? what have I done wrong? All the negative doubts and thoughts creep in and you begin to question who you are. I suppose in the thick of things you are never conscious of who you are when gripped with the pain and emotions of the events you experience. It is extremely difficult and almost impossible to see anything positive in yourself when faced with such traumas. Friends will be by your side and support you confirming that you are loved, appreciated, wanted and accepted. They will point out all the amazing values and attributes that make you who you are, but I guess the only people we want validation from are the ones that hurt us.

Only now can I see my value and worth in this life, after forty-seven years, that is a value and worth, I had to find in myself. No-one was ever going to give me that or provide that for me and that has perhaps been the biggest battle to overcome in recent years. Knowing in yourself that you are fucking amazing despite the events and adversity you go through is quite a peaceful place to be. Knowing that you do not need anyone to approve or validate your worth is truly peace within. Granted it is great when someone sees your worth and you value theirs too, but until you have that for yourself you will never be truly happy.

Everyone one of us has value and worth just being alive and breathing, is a value to the world. Each and everyone of us has a contribution to make to the world and I guess my journey I now see

191

my worth. Writing this book was my purpose in life not only for my daughter, but for everyone reading it. I trust that what I have shared has value, that you can apply to your own life in whatever way you choose. When you reach that place where you truly know who you are and what your purpose is you begin to know your worth. No-one can ever take that away from you. Your soul knows and that is all that matters.

"when you start to see your worth, you'll find it harder to stay around those who don't".

The Average Man

MEN

If you are reading this book which I guess only a few of you are then listen up. I do not care how bad you think you have messed up or who you think you are letting down at this moment in time, there is absolutely no shame at all in speaking your truth about how you might be feeling about things right now. Forget all this macho bullshit and lies we have been fed for hundreds of years about we do not show emotion and we need to be strong and dependable its all a crock of shit.

WAKE UP!

You need to be 100% vulnerable about anything you are feeling at this moment and speak from your heart. Do not let the ego protect you from being in your truth. **Anyone who does not see the value in you doing this should not be in your life**.

If you have been hiding something from your partner or wife, your parents, your friends, your kids and it's eating you up inside, then have that conversation with them. Do not live another day of your life suppressing your emotions and feelings just because you are living this subconscious programming and by a set of false beliefs. If you have past childhood trauma affecting you and it has for years, then it is time to deal with that, heal it so you can be the person you know you are. Like I said at the beginning of this book, it does not have to be a major trauma you need to release, it could be a simple belief that you are not loved or accepted in whatever area of your life, friends, work, career, a lover who cares what and who it's over, just release it and let it go.

Do not be afraid to cry do not be afraid to share you inner most thoughts and feelings. We all have a past, we all lie, we all do things we are not proud of and we all hurt people, we don't want to. Accept you are human, accept that you make mistakes, accept who you are and most of all, be comfortable about that. The people who love you and care about you want you to be happy and I know from bitter experience just how miserable holding on to all this baggage can be. Time to let it go Brother!.

The chances are that your feelings of self-worth are just negative based thoughts you hold onto because of an emotion attached to an experience unrealised at the time. The fact you are not conscious of it years later, only proves that you are living un consciously.

TRUTH AND AUTHENTICICTY

I wrote this book to get every **MAN** or woman who reads it to open up and speak their truth and come from a place of authenticity. To completely expose the truth of who you really are. Stop hiding behind the mask of who you want people to believe you are. It serves you, your wife, your partner, your kids, no purpose whatsoever to live in this falsehood for the rest of your days. Any suppressed emotions or feelings not dealt with will only catch up with you at some point. Hanging onto these has a detrimental effect on the body too. Duke Sayers relief from years of back pain only goes to show how impactful these suppressed feelings and emotions are having on the physiology and health of each and every one of us.

I want you to face the fear and step up as a soul of this world and tear the rule book up once and for all! We deserve to be loved, we deserve to be heard and we deserve to live authentically. We should not be forced to live with the belief that we need to be there for everyone else all the time. Everyone is ultimately responsible for their own happiness and spending your life trying to please others hoping that will be returned is a waste of time and energy. When you speak your truth and live in a place of authenticity, you will attract those people who will value this aspect of you, and you can be happy, loved, cherished, and have the good stuff in life. But the hard part is to get there, and this is all down to you and no one else.

My best friend of forty plus years has had a battle with family divorce far worse than mine and to this day is still battling for access to his kids, five years on and counting. He recently met a new partner and started to date but within months was finding the whole thing triggering and problematic. On a few occasions he was triggered into repeating old patterns of self-sabotaging and hitting the drink again. He had spent five years trying to fix himself. He came to me and said he said he could not see the relationship working and that both him and his new partner were too broken to come together from past pain and suffering, how could he fix it? They both wanted to be with each other but were both hiding behind the masks of the past. She was making all kinds of accusations that he was not telling her the truth about what he was dealing with and she was hiding her own secrets also. He was convinced that he was never going to make it work. I told him to speak his truth and lay it all out on the table for her to see, warts and all. With that he went to see her and took five years of court papers, transcripts, medical notes/ reports journals etc from his five-year battle following a very abusive and toxic divorce with his ex-wife. He gave this to his new partner and said, "that's me". He said if after you have read all that and you still want me then I will do my best to make this work. She spent three hours taking in my best mate's battle that had been officially documented over five years and she broke down in tears. She accepted him without conditions and felt more connected to him in that moment than she had been with anyone in her life, even her ex-husband of sixteen years.

If you are seeking a pure, genuine, and honest relationship with someone that you feel connected to and if it has any chance of success you need to speak your **truth**. You need to show **vulnerability** and you need to be **authentic** on every level. If the woman you want to be with accepts this about you, the only place you can go is forward in the knowledge that she has seen your soul, the mask is off, and you have nothing to hide behind.

He said it was the most terrifying thing to do and that his ego was fighting him all the time to not do it, but he knew it was the only way. I guess it was my turn to repay the favour to him when he had my back all those years ago.

This book is my truth, my vulnerability and I have battled my ego to share this story and journey with you. I know because of the last year I can no longer live my life without coming from a place of honesty, truth and living authentically. Besides the universe just simply will not allow that old me to return. I have a mission in life to guide others on their journeys and help them seek their own truths.

Seeing mine I hope to give you the inspiration to search for yours. Everything you are seeking answers to, lies within you, now just go and find it. Anyone who knows me and reads this book is without doubt going to form a judgement about it, and me for sharing this story and if it triggers you, angers you, offends you, makes you want to ask or raise a question or point of view about it then Its time you took a moment to look at who you really are. It's a reflection of something you need to address on the subconscious level.

"Truth is a point of view, but authenticity can't be faked".

Peter Gruber

ACKNOWLEDGEMENTS

There are far too many people I would like to acknowledge at this time but here are a few who have been key figures for me on my journey that deserve recognition for what they do to help others so selflessly.

My "SOUL TRIBE" and healing team

Duke Sayer - Thank you for the work that you do and for your impeccable and divine timing and the way you showed up in my life the way you did when I needed some direction. It was the universe that connected us, and had it not been for you and the team I am sure I would be in a very different place right now – Gratitude.

Yuggy Ramsay – It goes without saying your support and love for me during my journey has been nothing short of unwavering. – Gratitude.

Ines Lopez – Your guidance and advice on all things spiritual when I struggled to understand parts of my journey and what it all meant - Gratitude.

Mark Goddard – Another brave man who has been on his journey and offered pearls of wisdom and light in times of dark despondency – Gratitude.

Chloe Virginia – For allowing me to be an emotional wreck during a call we had together- your compassion for others has no bounds - Gratitude.

Jagunath Sva – Thank you for the experiential healing process and guided meditation you gave me at a time I was beginning to question this journey – Gratitude.

CONCIOUS COMMUNITY

There are simply too many of you to list here but each and everyone of you has shown me unconditional love, unwavering support, and flashes of inspiration and gratitude during my journey. I am humbled to be a part of a collective of people that have truly inspired me to be the very best version of myself when I thought it was not possible to turn my life around. Your love and compassion for others, as a collective, has been a blessing to be a part of, and I have the utmost love and respect to also see how far all of you have come on your own journeys over the last year. I guess I have a "new attachment" and that is to be a part of this community for as long as I need to be. It is one attachment I consciously do not want to release!

FAMILY

To all my family who have given me the experiences both good and bad over the years that have made me the person I am today. I thank you for these experiences and what I have learnt from them. I know and understand that some of you perhaps do not quite understand me as you once did and that I am now a very person in a lot of aspects. I don't expect to fully get where I am coming from now, but that's OK.

FRIENDS

To my best friend and "brother from another mother"! We have been there for each other all our lives and I know that will never change. We have both been on a similar journey in recent years and although each of our journeys has been very different, they're aligned in our growth of who we are in this very moment. I am truly grateful to have you in my life and I love you man!

REFERENCES

Throughout my journey I spent much time watching youtube videos and listening to podcasts from some truly amazing people all of whom contributed either directly through courses or indirectly through words of inspiration. The understanding and clarity of which these people speak are all based on their own life's journey and experiences very much like mine. I trust you will take some time to listen to what these people have to say and take what you can form the lessons they offer.

Duker Sayer	https://dukesayer.com
Rebecca Adams	https://rebeccaadamsbiz.com
James Boardman	https://www.boardmanjames.com /
Kyle Cease	https://kylecease.com
David Goggins	https://davidgoggins.com
Eckhart Tolle	https://eckharttolle.com

Feedback / reviews

I would love to hear from you if this book has resonated with you on any level and you have had your own realisations or awakened thoughts on aspects on your life from me sharing my story.

Please feel free to email me.

theaveragebrokenman@gmail.com

LOVE & LIGHT TO ALL THOSE WHO DO THE WORK!

THANK YOU

JOURNAL & NOTES

The remainder of this book is for your notes - Please take ten minutes each day to sit in silence, close your eyes and meditate. Breathe deep into your body and be at one with your breath. Journal your feelings about childhood, teenage years, love, family friends, or whatever shows up for you. Take the time to reflect and think about those moments in your life good or bad and see what you can discover about the **REAL YOU**.

MEDITATION NOTES: Date: Time:

MEDITATION NOTES:

MEDITATION NOTES:

MEDITATION NOTES:

MEDITATION NOTES:

MEDITATION NOTES:

MEDITATION NOTES:

MEDITATION NOTES:

MEDITATION NOTES:

MEDITATION NOTES:

MEDITATION NOTES:

MEDITATION NOTES:

MEDITATION NOTES:

MEDITATION NOTES:

MEDITATION NOTES:

MEDITATION NOTES:

MEDITATION NOTES:

MEDITATION NOTES:

MEDITATION NOTES:

MEDITATION NOTES:

MEDITATION NOTES:

MEDITATION NOTES:

MEDITATION NOTES:

MEDITATION NOTES:

MEDITATION NOTES:

MEDITATION NOTES:

MEDITATION NOTES:

MEDITATION NOTES:

MEDITATION NOTES:

MEDITATION NOTES:

MEDITATION NOTES:

MEDITATION NOTES: